# Grand Rapids
## *Night After Night*

the photography of Brian Kelly

Copyright © 2000 Brian Kelly

Published 2000 by
Glass Eye
P.O. Box 1811
Grand Rapids, Michigan 49501-1811

First edition/First printing June 2000.

Photographs © 2000 by Brian Kelly
Introduction © 2000 by Mayor John H. Logie
Essay © 2000 by Jonathon Russell
All other written text © 2000 by Brian Kelly

All rights reserved. No part of this publication may be reproduced, stored in a retrieval system, or transmitted in any form or by any means, including motion picture film, video, electronic, mechanical, photocopying, recording or otherwise, without the prior permission in writing from the publisher and the individual copyright owners.

Printed by Singer Printing - Petaluma, California
Edited by Kathleen Kelly and Joseph Milanowski
Art Direction by Brian Kelly and Kathleen Kelly
Graphic Design by Bryan Graham

Library of Congress Cataloging in Publication Data:
Kelly, Brian 1968-
Grand Rapids: Night After Night/Brian Kelly
        p.cm.
1. Photography, Artistic. 2. Grand Rapids, Michigan. 3. Kelly, Brian.    I. Title

ISBN 0-9701293-0-0

10 9 8 7 6 5 4 3 2 1

Printed and bound in the United States of America

# INTRODUCTION

I first met Brian Kelly in February, 1997, at a reception for the re-opening of the Amway Grand Plaza Hotel's Bentham's Restaurant in Grand Rapids, Michigan. The hotel, in order to accent the newly remodeled restaurant, had acquired numerous photographic images from Brian's portfolio. I was immediately struck by how his photographs captured the essence of the historic river that flows through downtown Grand Rapids, thereby complementing the restaurant's urban riverfront location. These images impressed me unlike any I had previously seen of downtown Grand Rapids and the Grand River.

As I talked with Brian over the course of that evening, and in many subsequent encounters, I learned of his profound passion for the City of Grand Rapids. This passion is one he shares not only with me, but also with the many talented individuals who are presently changing the face of our City and driving the explosive revitalization and growth Grand Rapids has enjoyed over the last decade. Brian's photographs celebrate that growth and visually interpret a City that is diverse, vibrant and full of life.

Brian Kelly has made Grand Rapids a major setting for his life's work and it is fortunate that he continues to explore this urban landscape with his camera. Because, as he does, we all begin to see a "Grand" city in ways not even imagined before, a truly unique experience in my eyes. The images created from his explorations into the City at night reveal to us a Grand Rapids we have never before seen. Or, if we have, we soon realize we have never seen it quite like he does.

I look back now to my first conversation with Brian and find myself pleased to have shared with him an important evening in his career. In the few years since that reception at Bentham's, I have encountered Brian's artwork in places all around the City. From the Grand Rapids Art Museum, to the Van Andel Museum Center, to the Urban Institute for Contemporary Art, and in both private and corporate collections, this City has embraced his work. Brian's unique style is unmistakable and immediately recognizable in its excellence; a characteristic shared by all great artists.

Brian Kelly - one of Grand Rapids' most treasured artists. I invite you to turn the pages of this book and witness what he has seen.

*Mayor John H. Logie*
*City of Grand Rapids, June 2000*

# Essay

When I first met Brian Kelly he was enrolled in a photography class that I was teaching at Grand Rapids Community College. Brian was one of those special students that all educators feel privileged to encounter during their careers; one passionately seeking what their chosen medium can reveal, not willing to settle, but wanting to fully explore a visual concept. Brian, with this book, has taken a concept and turned it into a lasting and handsome statement.

Photography, more than any other art form, allows the artist to use Time as a creative element. The photographer may present Time to the viewer as a fraction of a second, arresting objects in motion, or convey multiple seconds, minutes or hours in a single exposure, all reveal to us a world that we are not physically able to see. The creative control of Time is one of the major attractions of photography. Brian Kelly presents to us another dimension of Grand Rapids by his unique use of nocturnal time exposures.

Brian's photographs show us that night is not the reverse of day; black surfaces and white are not merely reversed, as on a sheet of film, but another world altogether emerges at night. Water, due to a long exposure, may become a surface of silver. Streaks of light on a roadway show the passing of traffic; streaks of light in the heavens become star trails. Sometimes the world is in motion on a level that we can easily see, and sometimes it moves on a level that is so subtle that only a long photographic exposure can record it. Brian's images remind us that our world is in constant motion.

When viewing the work of an accomplished artist in any medium of expression, the artwork presented to the audience may look effortless. Brian's images look effortless. Technically, however, Brian's images are not easy to master. It is not simply a matter of which f-stop and shutter speed are needed for the correct exposure, but more importantly, "What is the element of Time doing creatively?" Brian has previsualized his compositions or, said another way, seen ahead of Time. The moving traffic lights, waving flags, star trails or water that turns into liquid silver can only be seen in the Artist's imagination.

Are Brian Kelly's images within the pages of this book to be considered great? To quote Ansel Adams, a man whom I had the good fortune to know and study with:

> "A great photograph is a full expression of what one feels about what is being photographed in the deepest sense, and is, thereby, a true expression of what one feels about life in its entirety. The expression of what one feels should be set forth in terms of simple devotion to the medium."

Brian Kelly's simple devotion to the photographic medium has allowed us a new vision of Grand Rapids.

*Jonathon Russell, June 2000*

Jonathon Russell came to Grand Rapids, Michigan to start the Photography Program at Grand Rapids Community College. The photography program he began in 1978 is now known as a national leader in photographic education. Many of the program's students are ranked in the top five percent of all two-year and four-year college level photography students nationally. Russell has studied with such notables as Ansel Adams and Brett Weston. His photographic images are found in private, corporate and museum collections worldwide. He continues to teach and mentor students in the program he began over twenty years ago at Grand Rapids Community College.

# Acknowledgements

*For my wife Kathleen & daughter Hanna*

I must thank my parents, Gordon and Susan Kelly, for their guidance, support and encouragement. It is because of their continuous faith and hope that my life has become what it is today.

My appreciation to Mayor John H. Logie, for his kind letter of introduction and tireless commitment to the City of Grand Rapids. Without his efforts, there would be less to photograph.

I am grateful to Jonathon Russell, for his eloquent essay and contribution to this book. I admire his photographic honesty and professionalism. He is a wonderful educator and mentor to all of us who have studied with him.

To Hank and Diane Milanowski, for always having a bottomless pot of Traverse City Cherry coffee brewing. Your kindness and generosity have warmed me more than your coffee.

To the makers of Diet Pepsi and Hot Tamales, your ingredients have kept many late night photography sessions going until sunrise (I receive no sponsorships from named products…hint, hint).

Thank you to Bill Schwab, whose own wonderful book was a catalyst for mine. I value your friendship and willingness to share what you have learned.

I need to thank in some abstract way, the City of Grand Rapids herself. *Night After Night*, I would head out into the darkness searching for something yet to be known. You have always rewarded my efforts, and provided endless amounts of adventure around every corner.

My appreciation to the Frederik Meijer Gardens for allowing me after-hours admission to their grounds and access to their unbelievable bronze horse.

I would like to express my deep appreciation to several key philanthropic families and individuals that are time and again exceedingly generous when asked to help create exciting new projects that enrich our city. I would have liked to name you all here, but for fear of leaving anyone off the list, I will let the previous statement stand for itself.

This project has been an exciting journey; I look forward to what the future may bring.

*Brian Kelly, June 2000*

plate one   River Arches, 1998

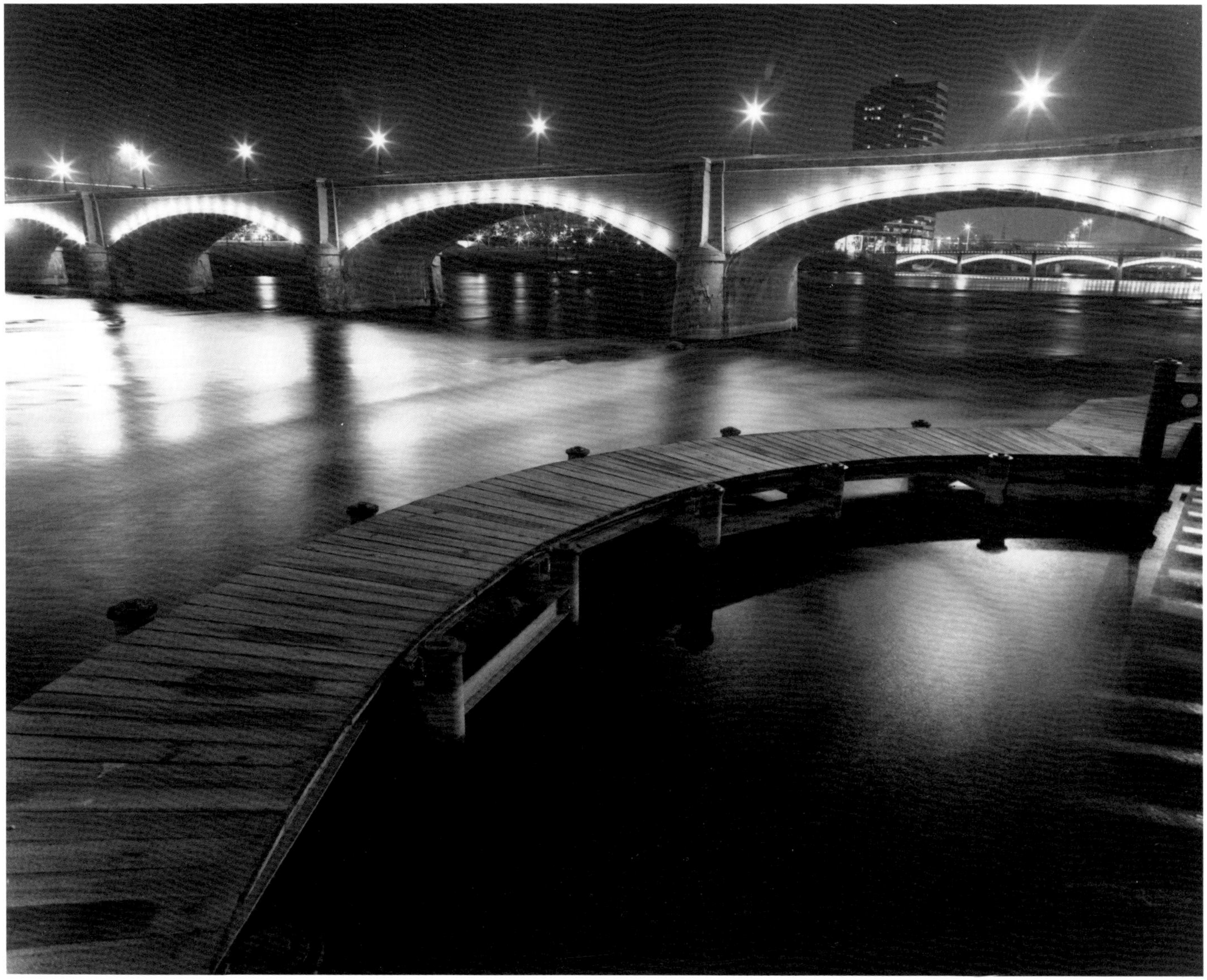

plate two   River Abstract, 1998

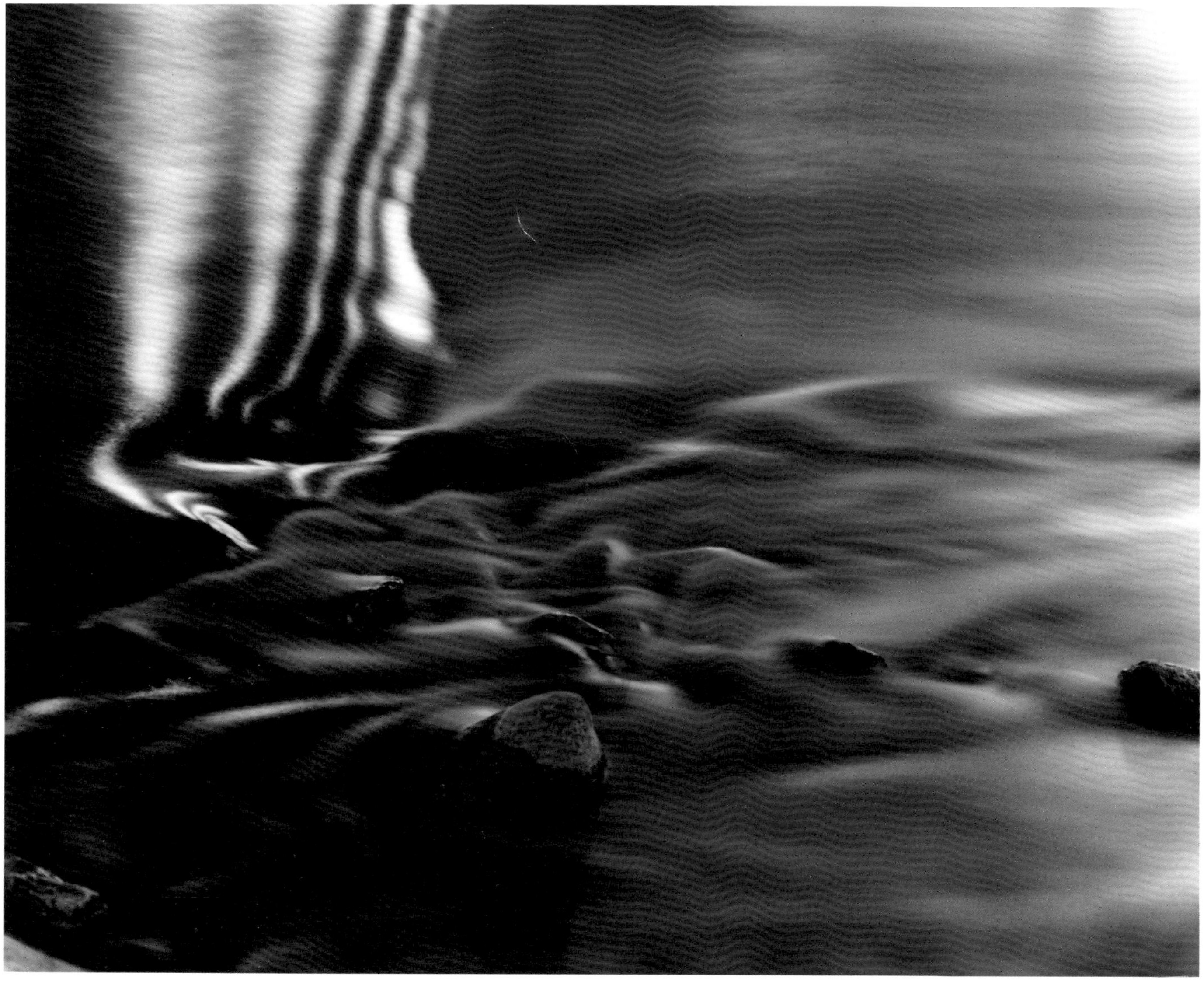

plate three   Fish Ladder, Sixth Street Bridge, 1996

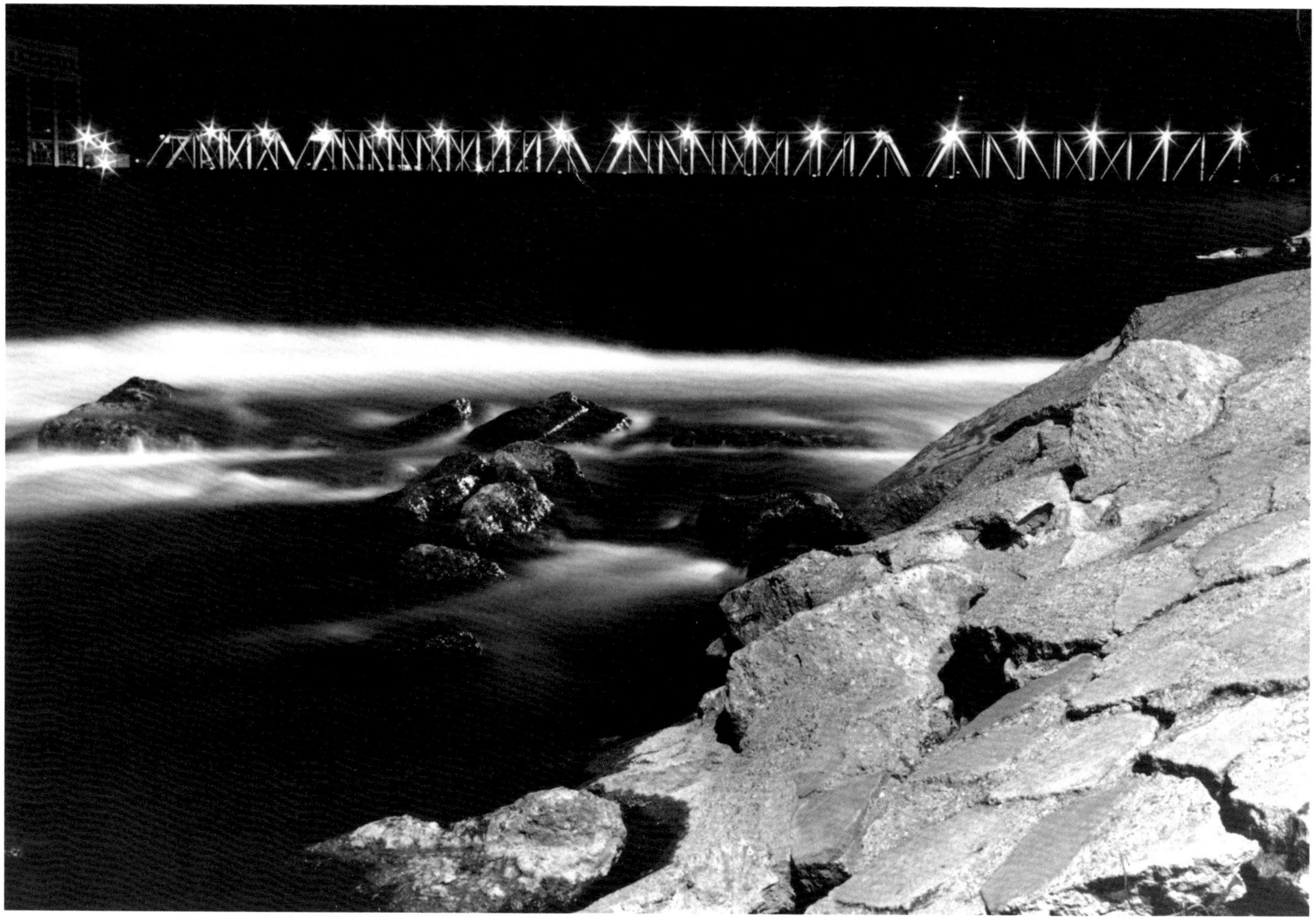

plate four    South View One, 1996

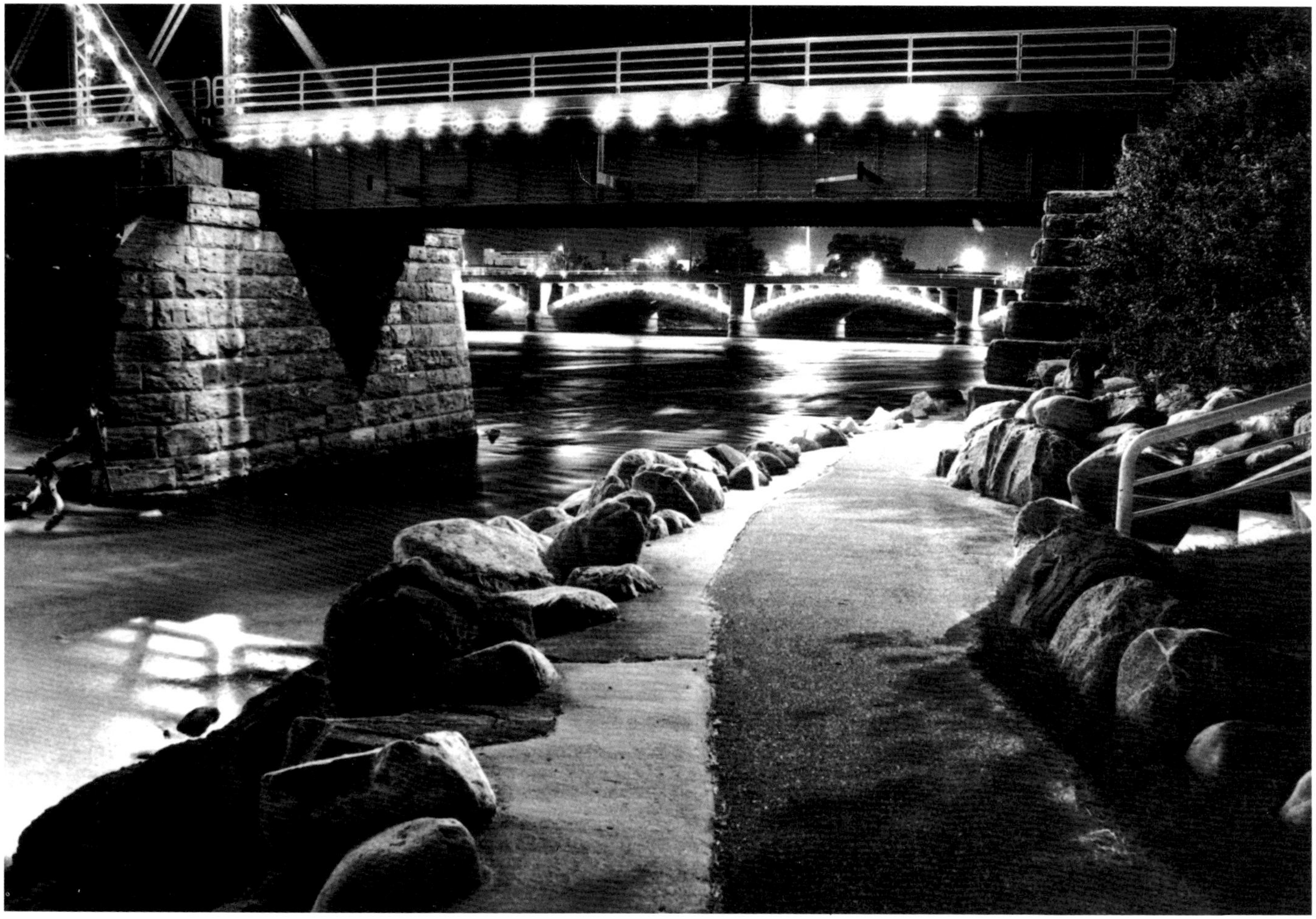

plate five   Lamp Post - Van Andel Public Museum, 1998

plate six   Calder Abstract, 2000

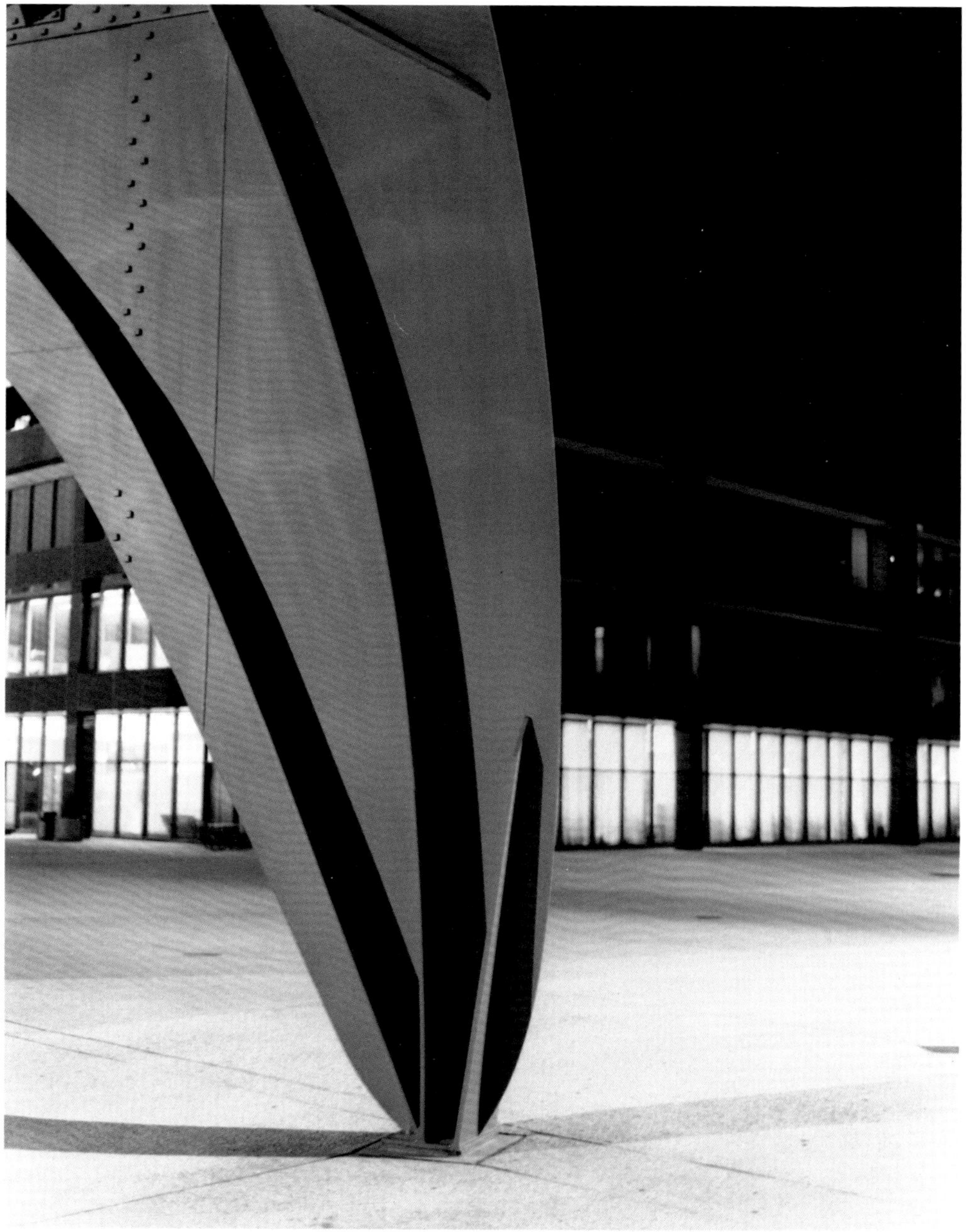

plate seven   Glowing Pillars - Bridgewater Place, 2000

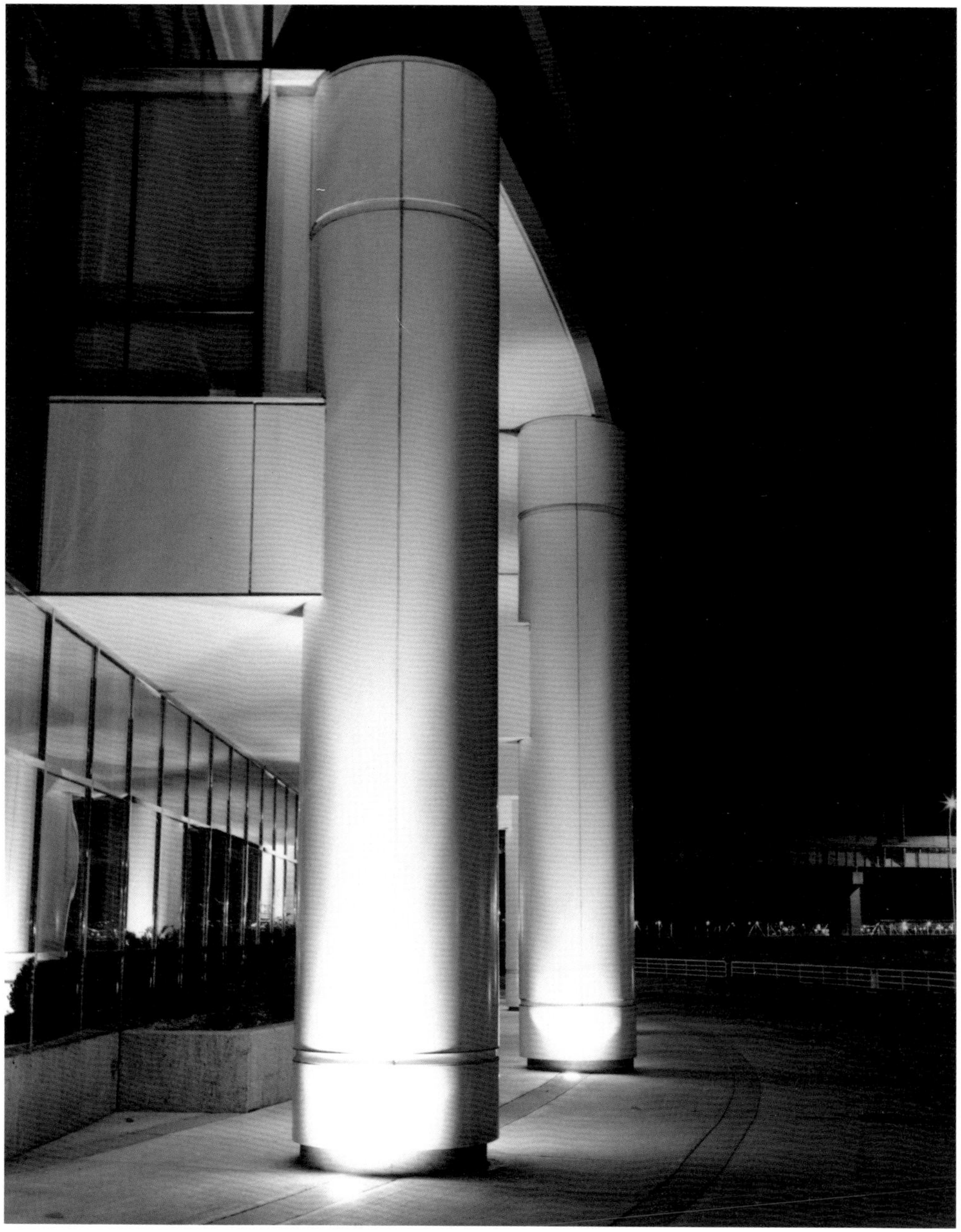

plate eight   Steam Cloud, Star Trails - Bridgewater Place, 2000

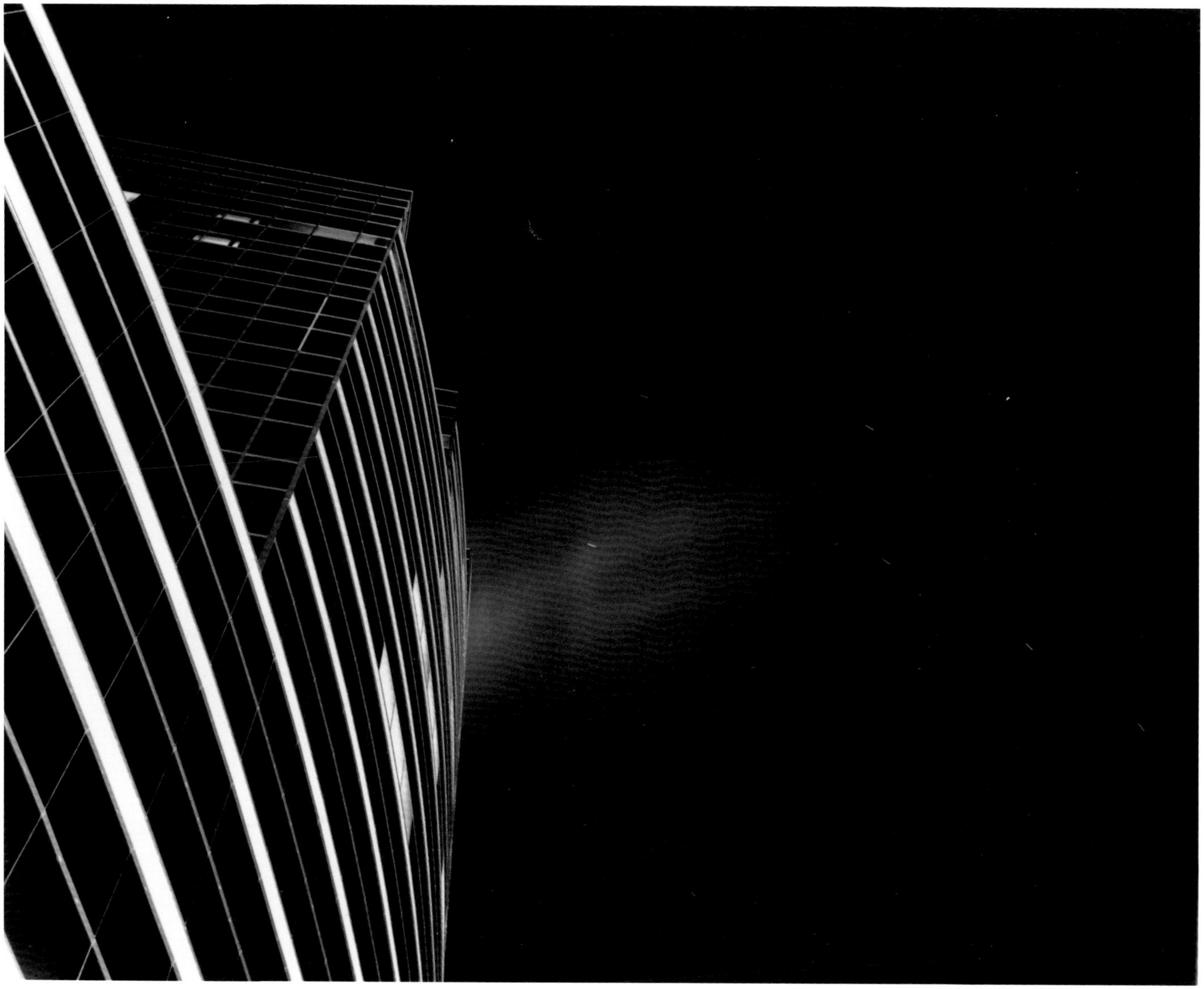

plate nine   Crescent Moon and Van Andel Arena, 1996

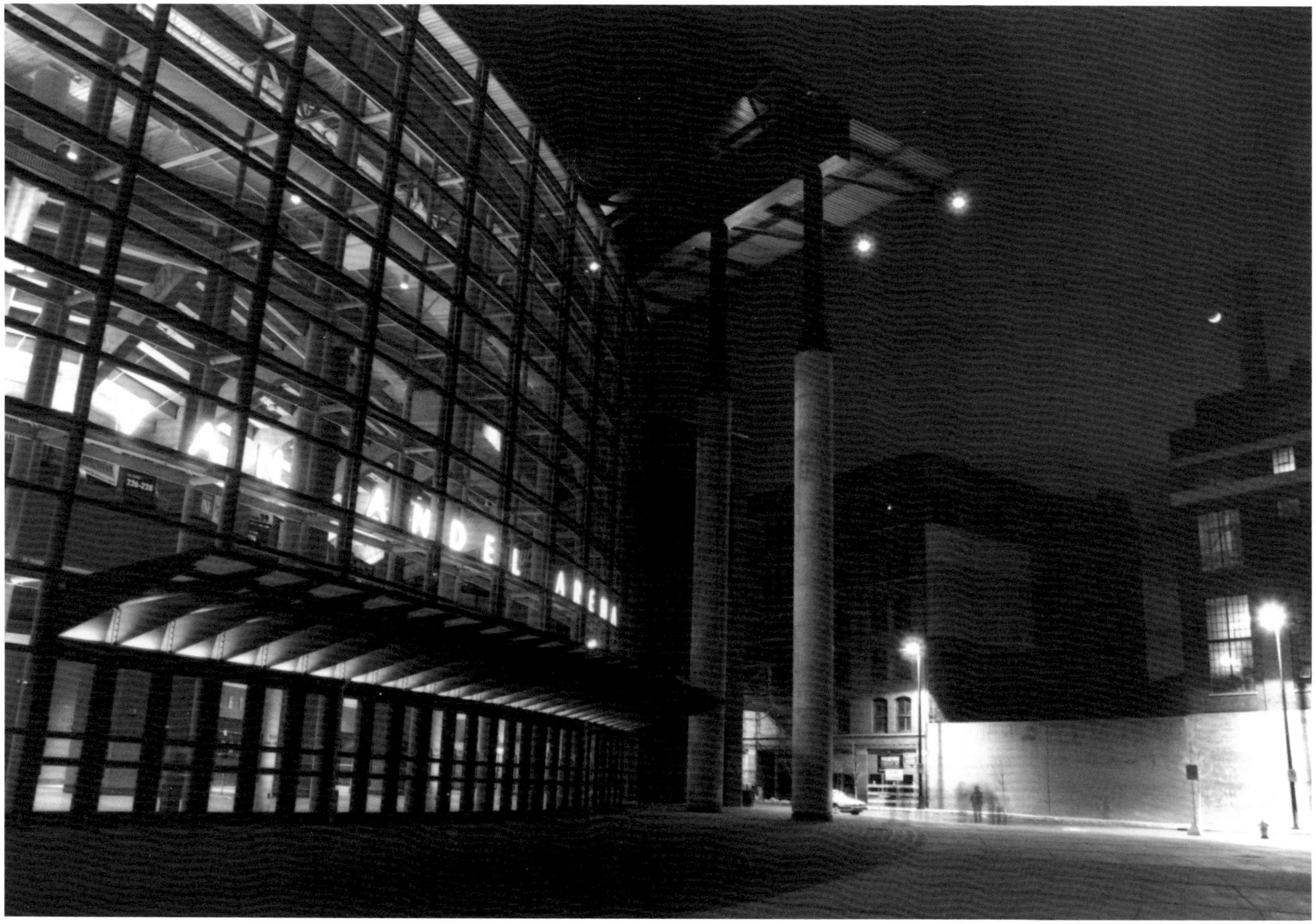
ANDEL ARENA

plate ten   Van Andel Arena - Aerial, 1998

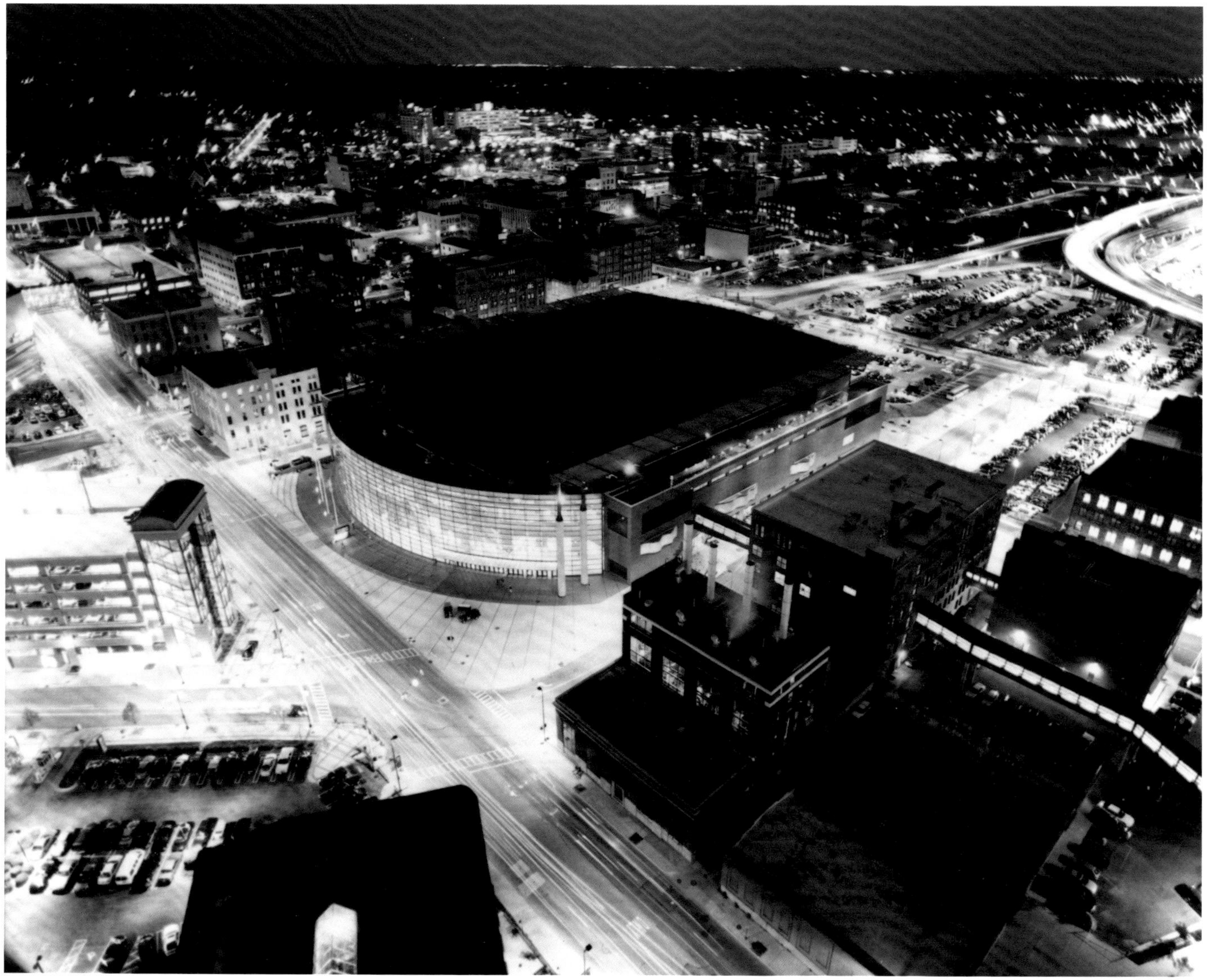

plate eleven   Van Andel Public Museum - Aerial, 1998

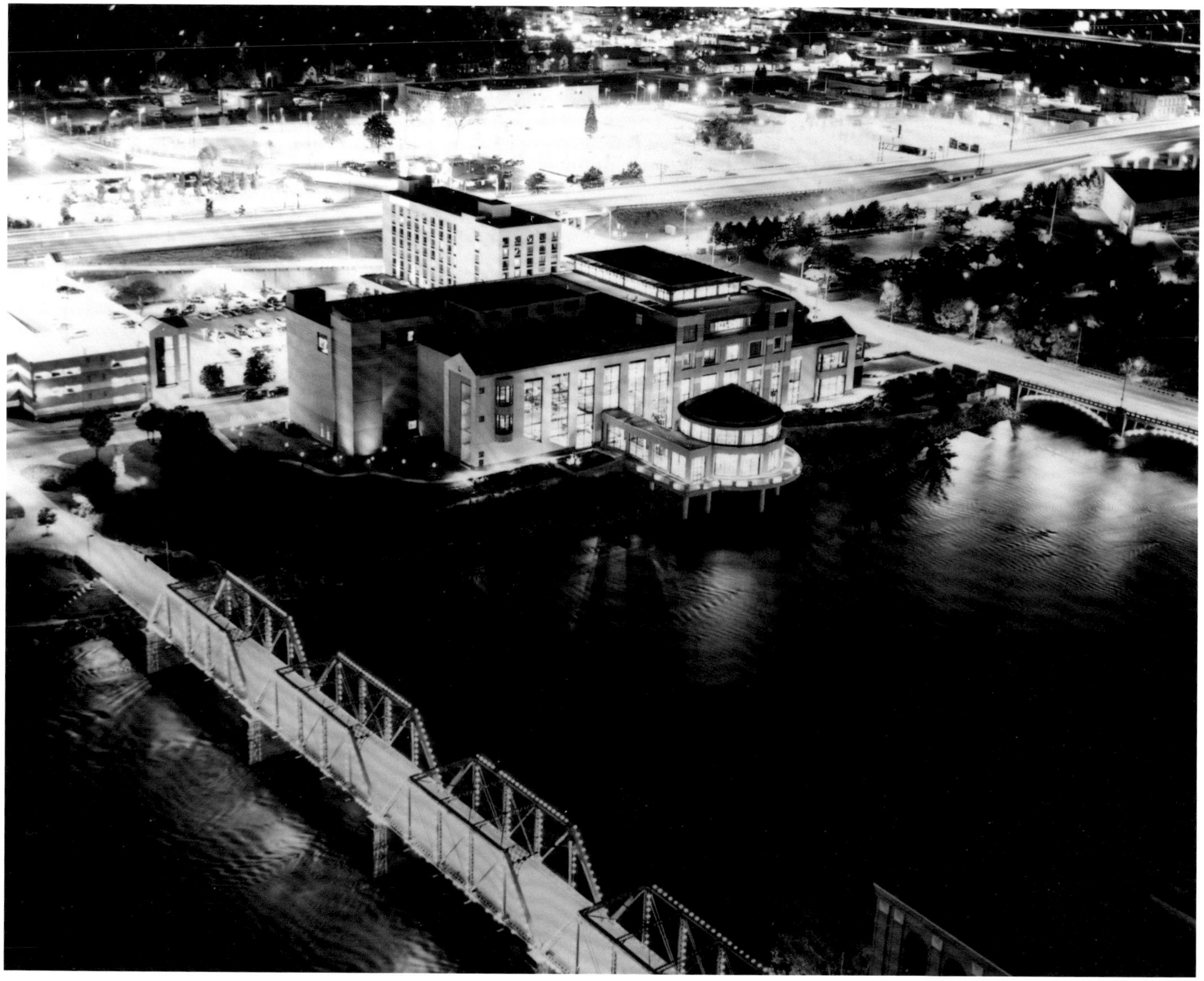

plate twelve    Under Pearl Street Bridge and Van Andel Museum, 2000

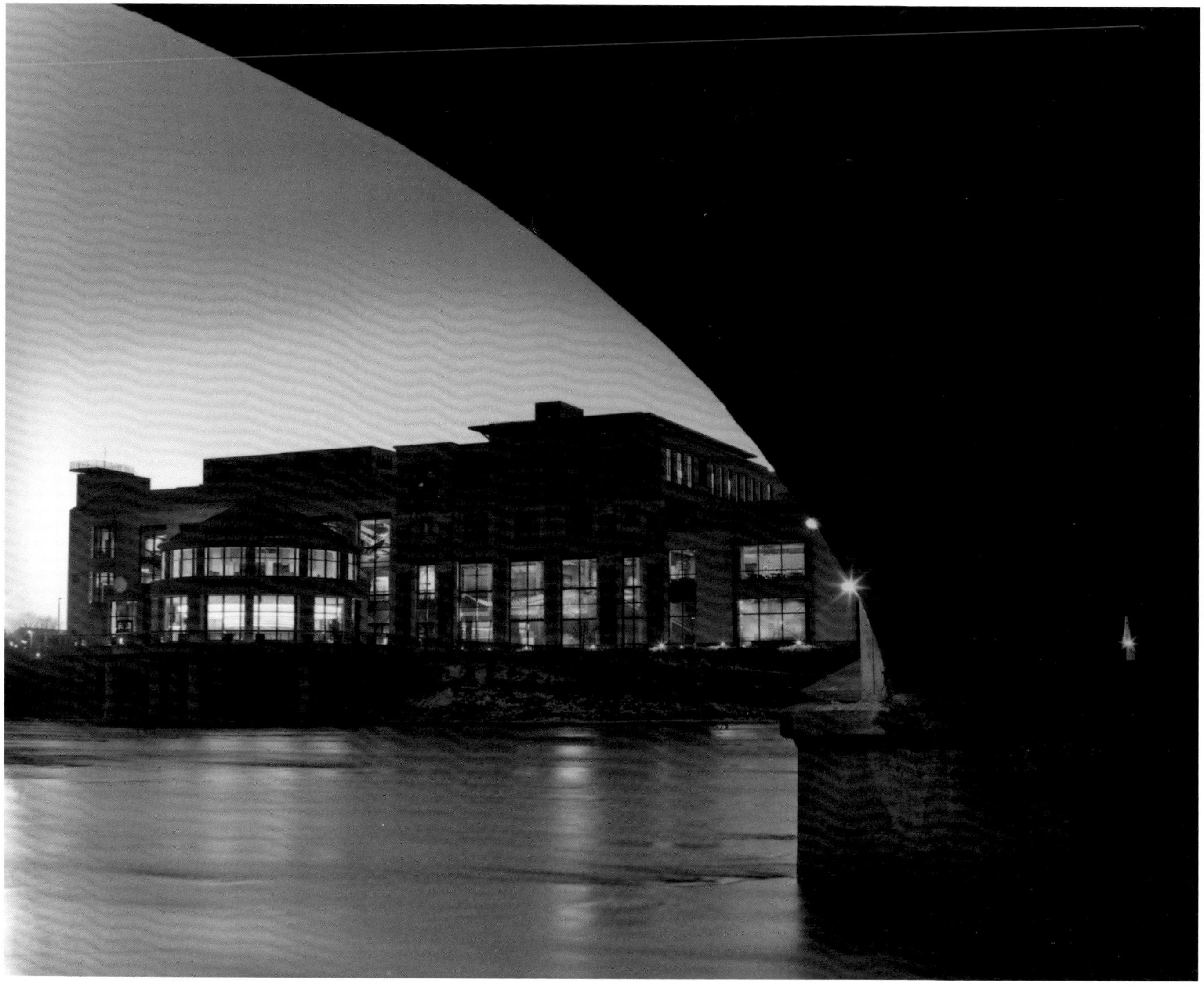

plate thirteen   Six Trees - Van Andel Institute, 2000

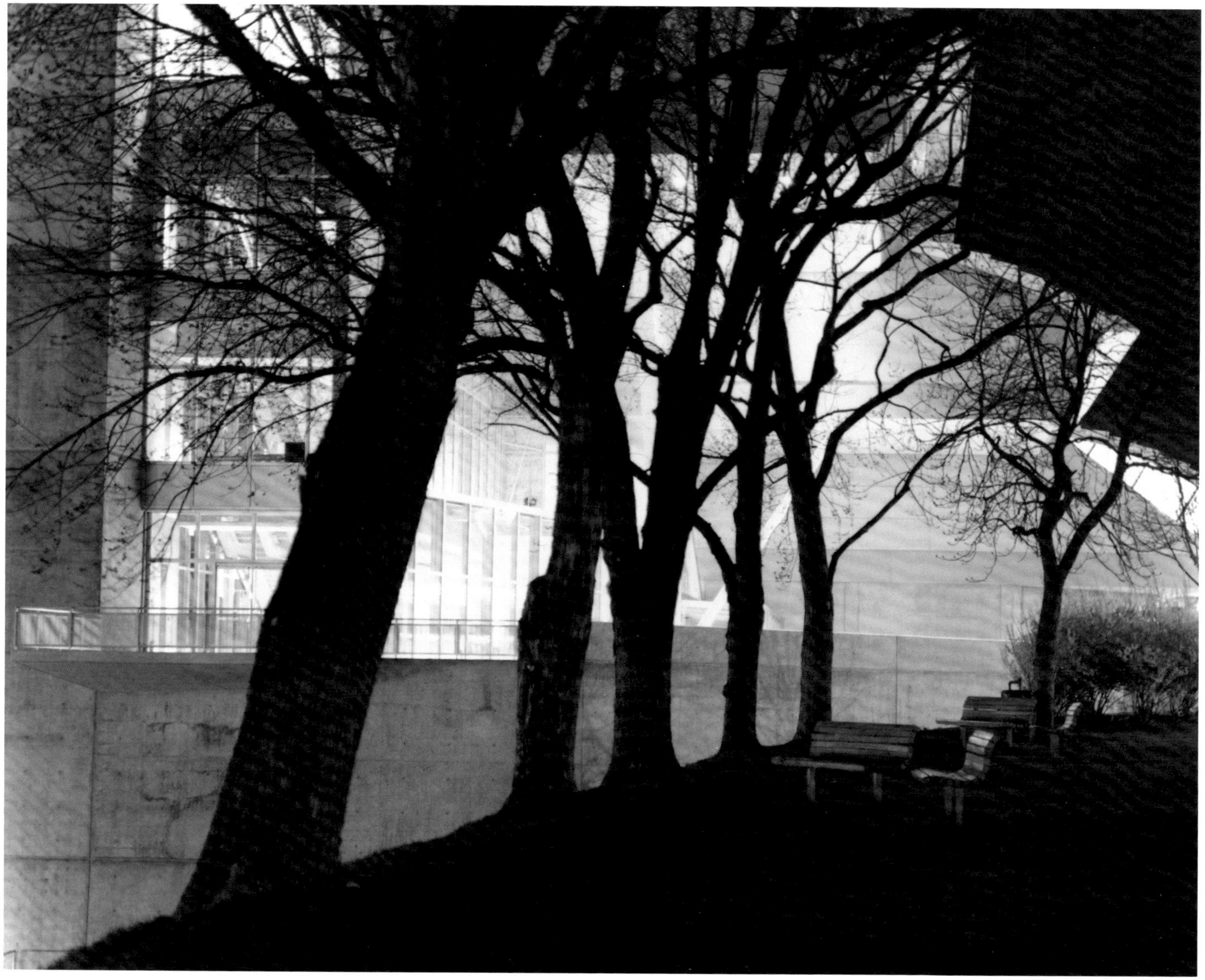

plate fourteen   Nine Flags - Amway World Headquarters, 2000

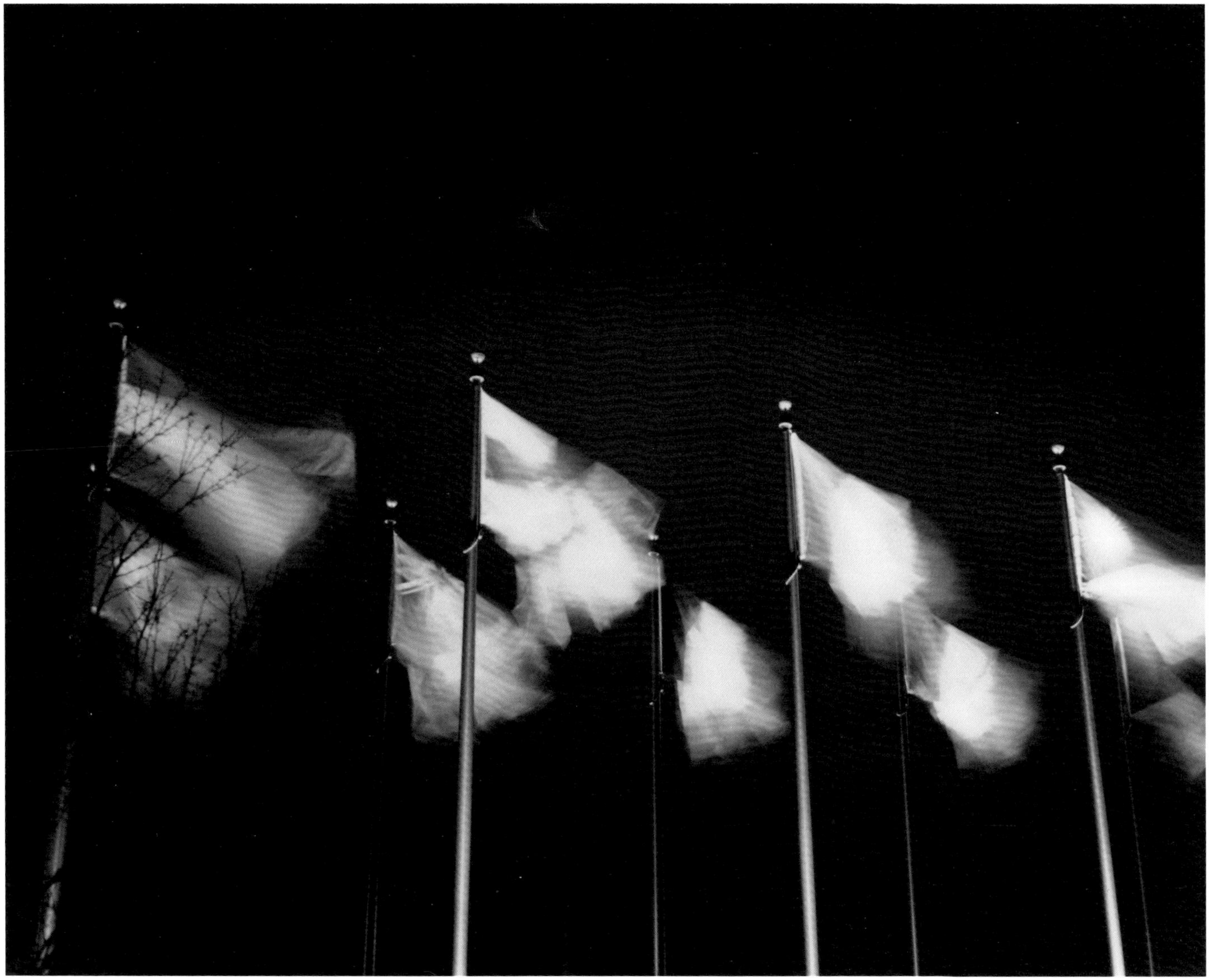

plate fifteen   Lamp Post, Covered Bridge - Ada, 2000

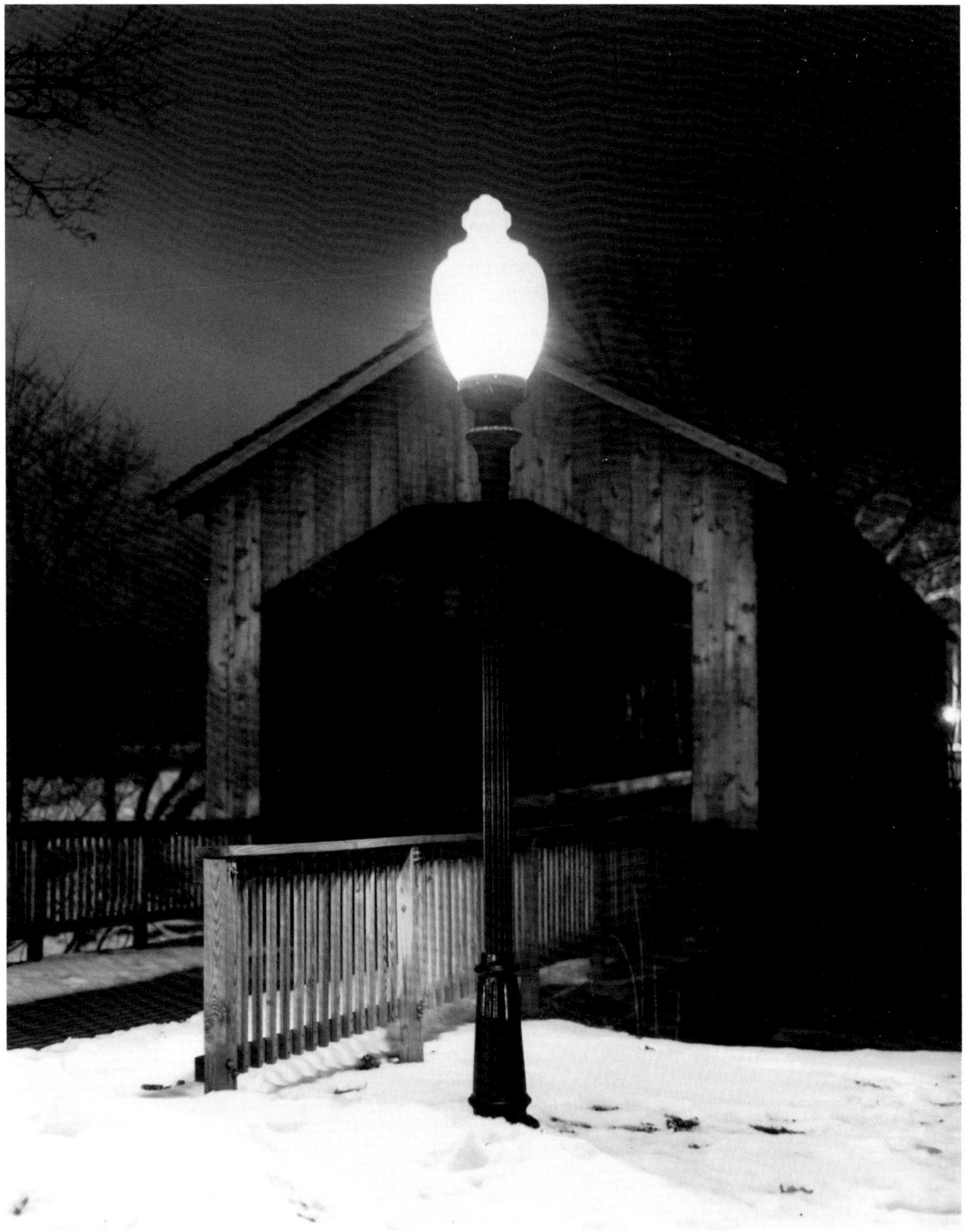

plate sixteen   Tree and Blue Bridge, 2000

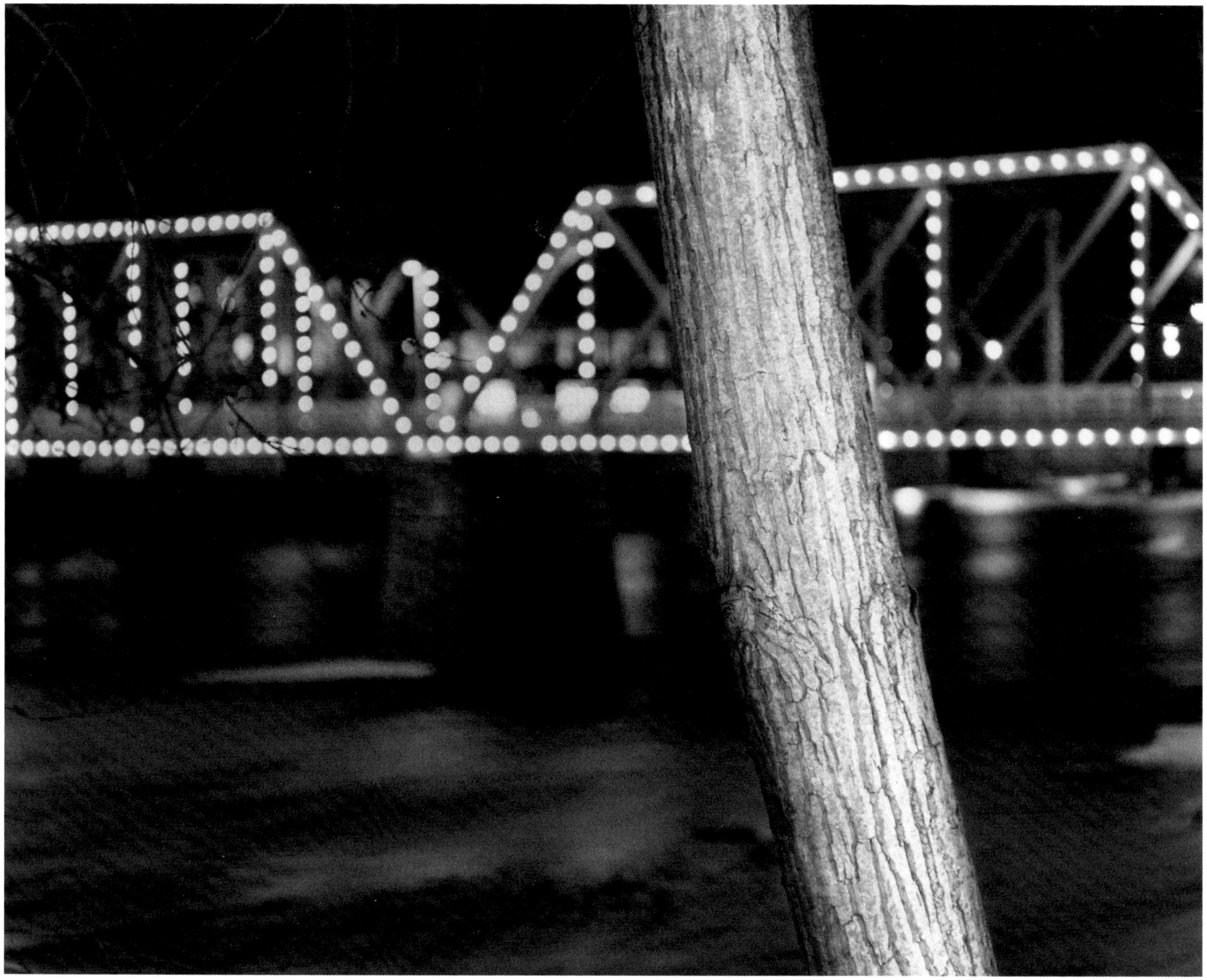

plate seventeen   Illuminated Trees - Collins Park, EGR, 2000

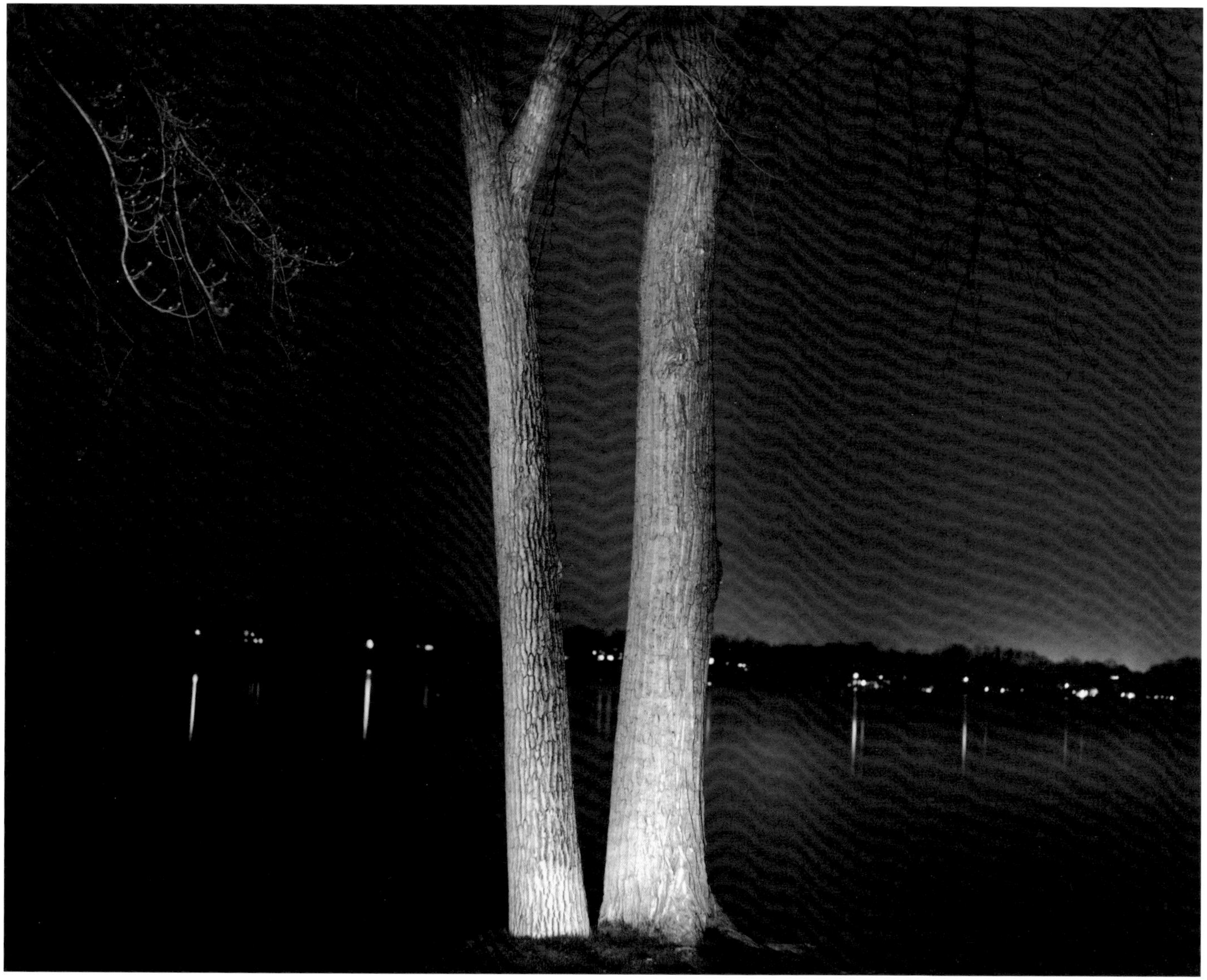

plate eighteen   Wet Sidewalk - Gerald R. Ford Museum, 1998

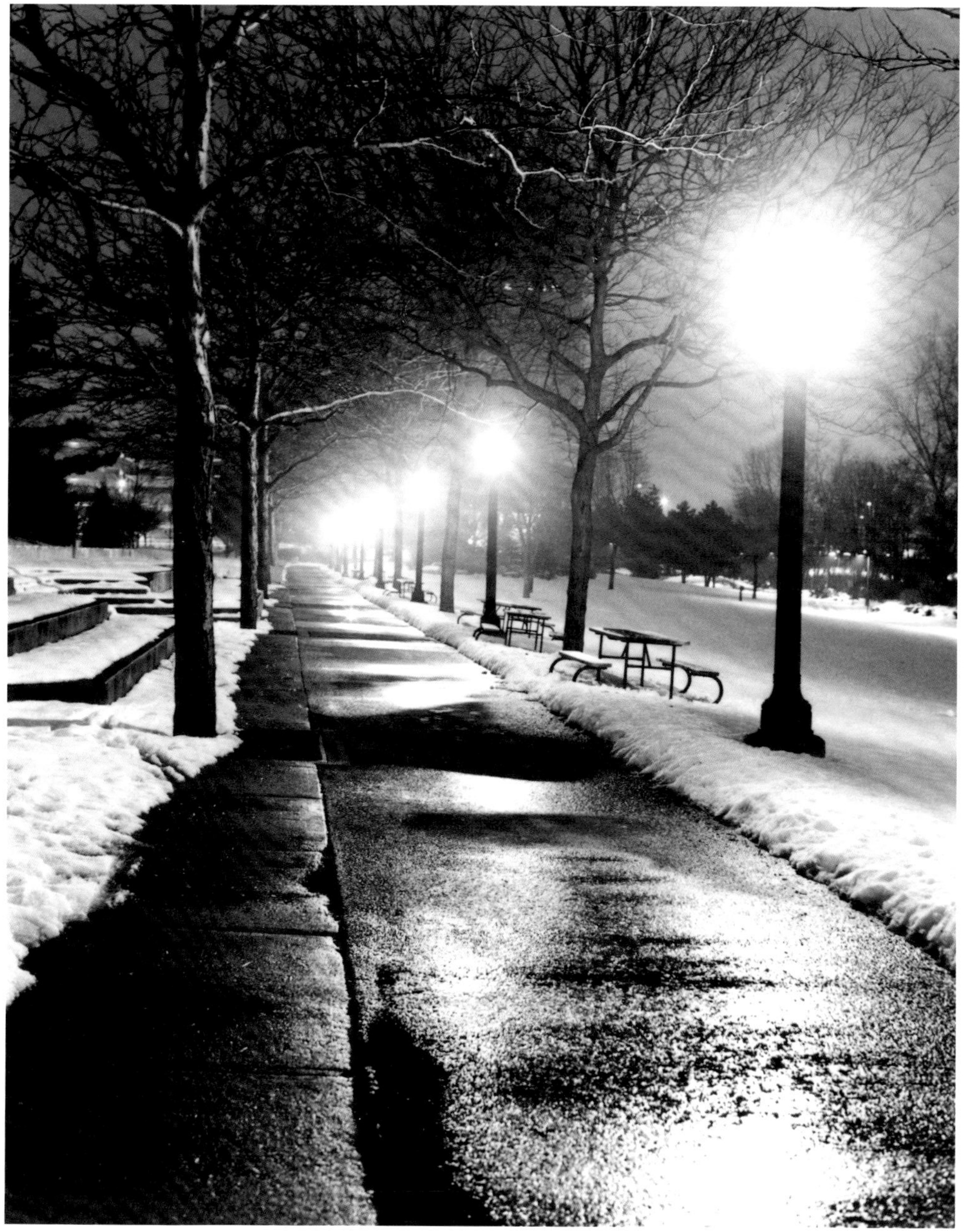

plate nineteen   Five Arches, 1999

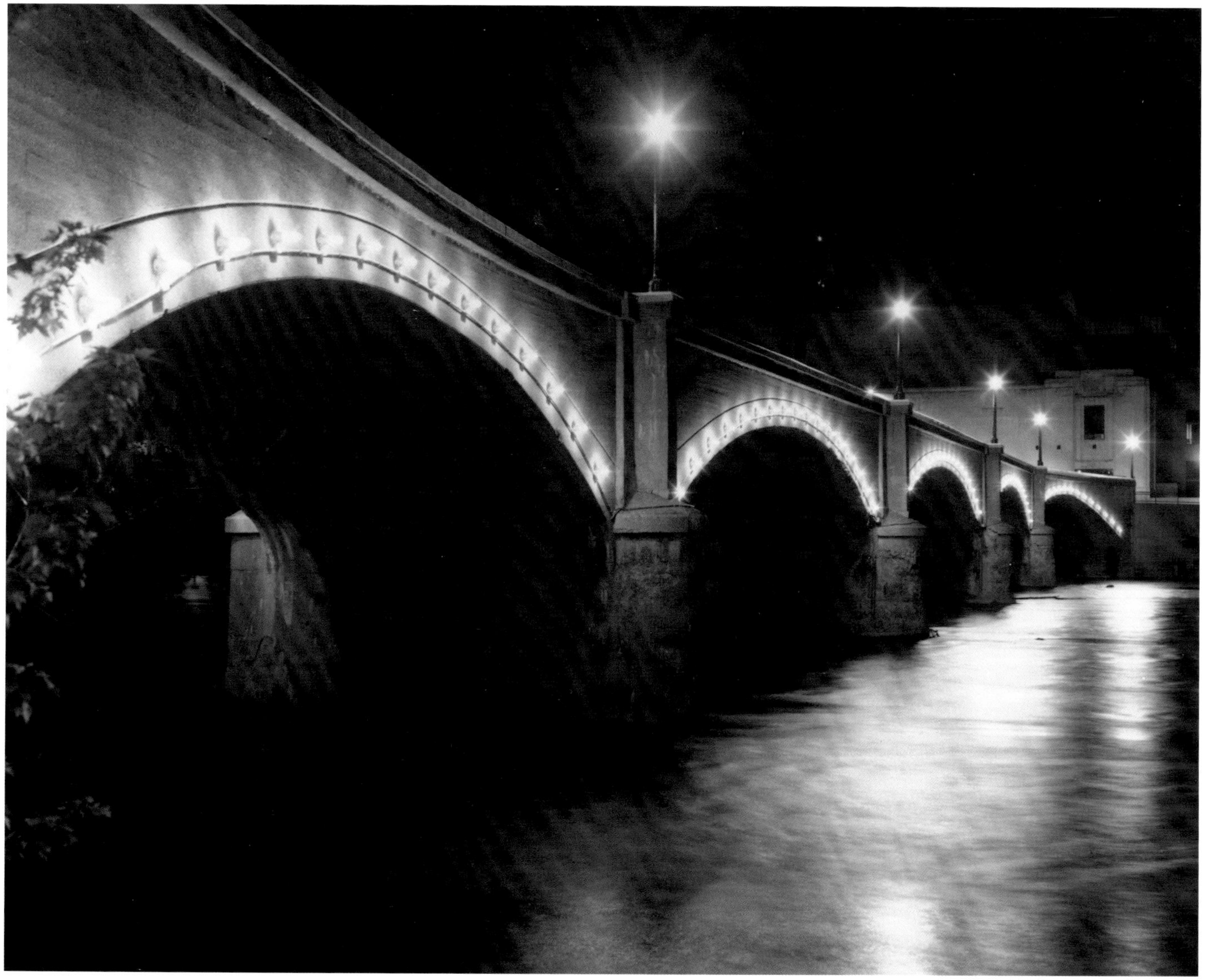

plate twenty   Passing Bike and Monroe Café, 2000

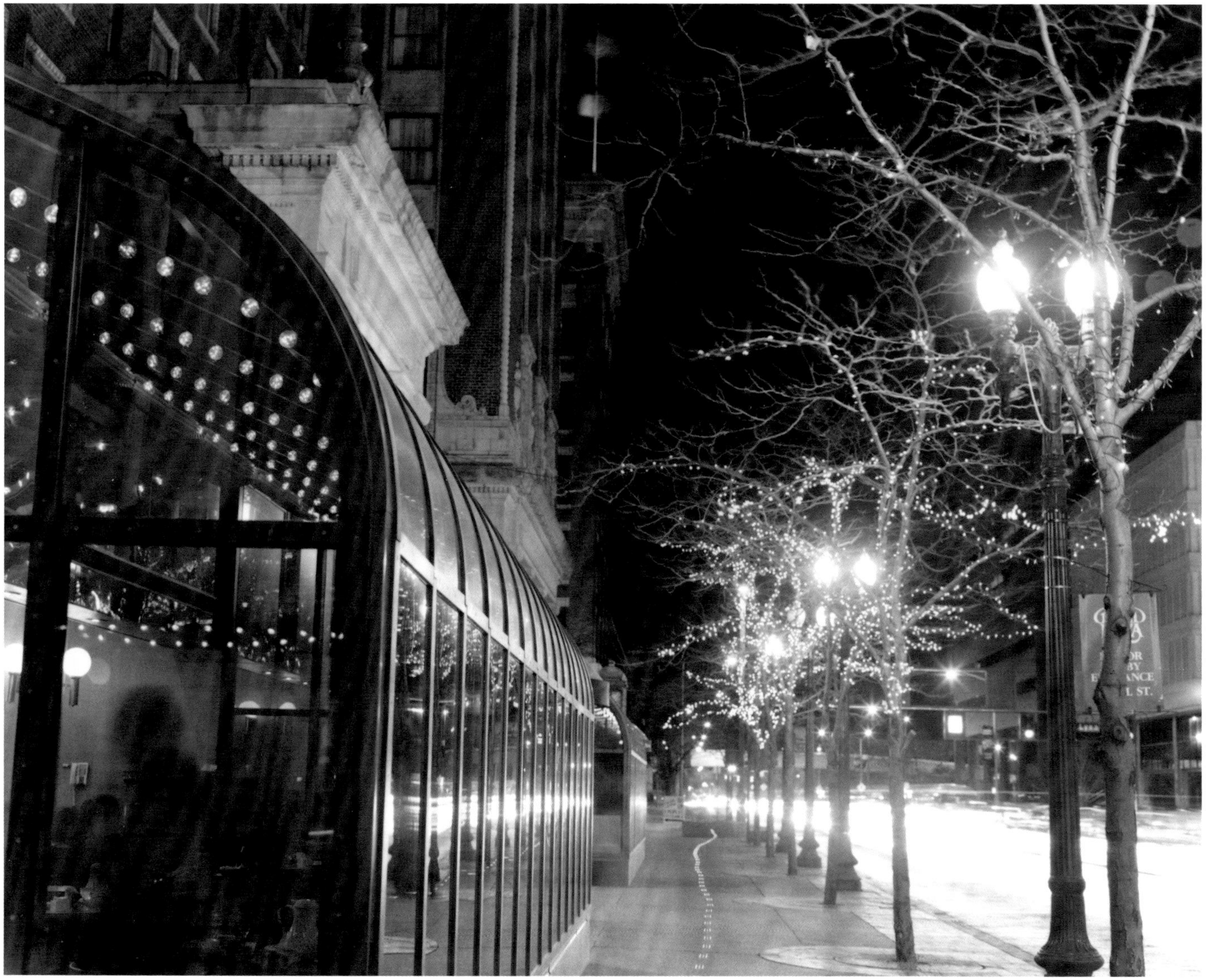

plate twenty-one    Moon and Amway Grand Plaza Hotel, 2000

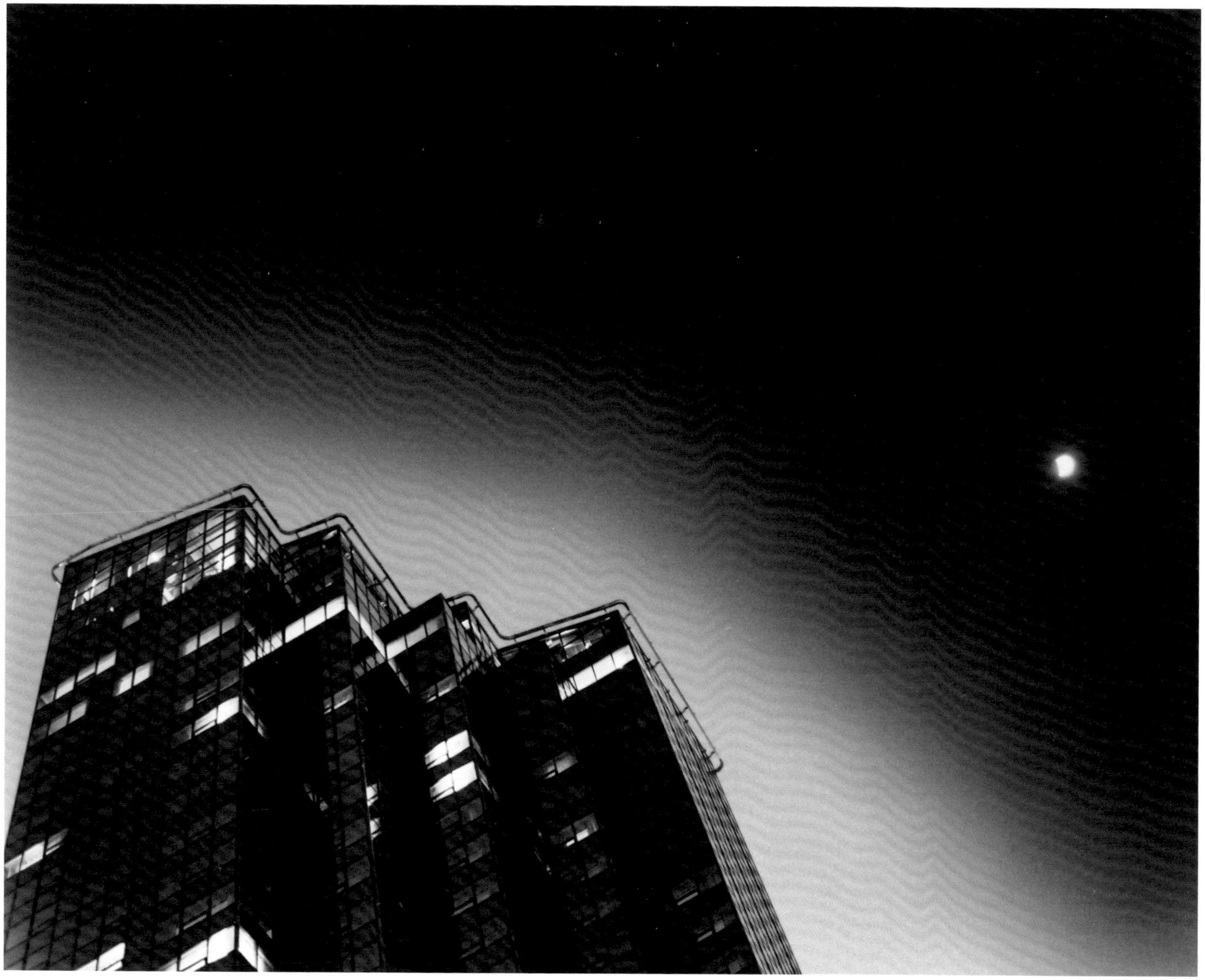

plate twenty-two   Star Trails and Steelcase Pyramid, 2000

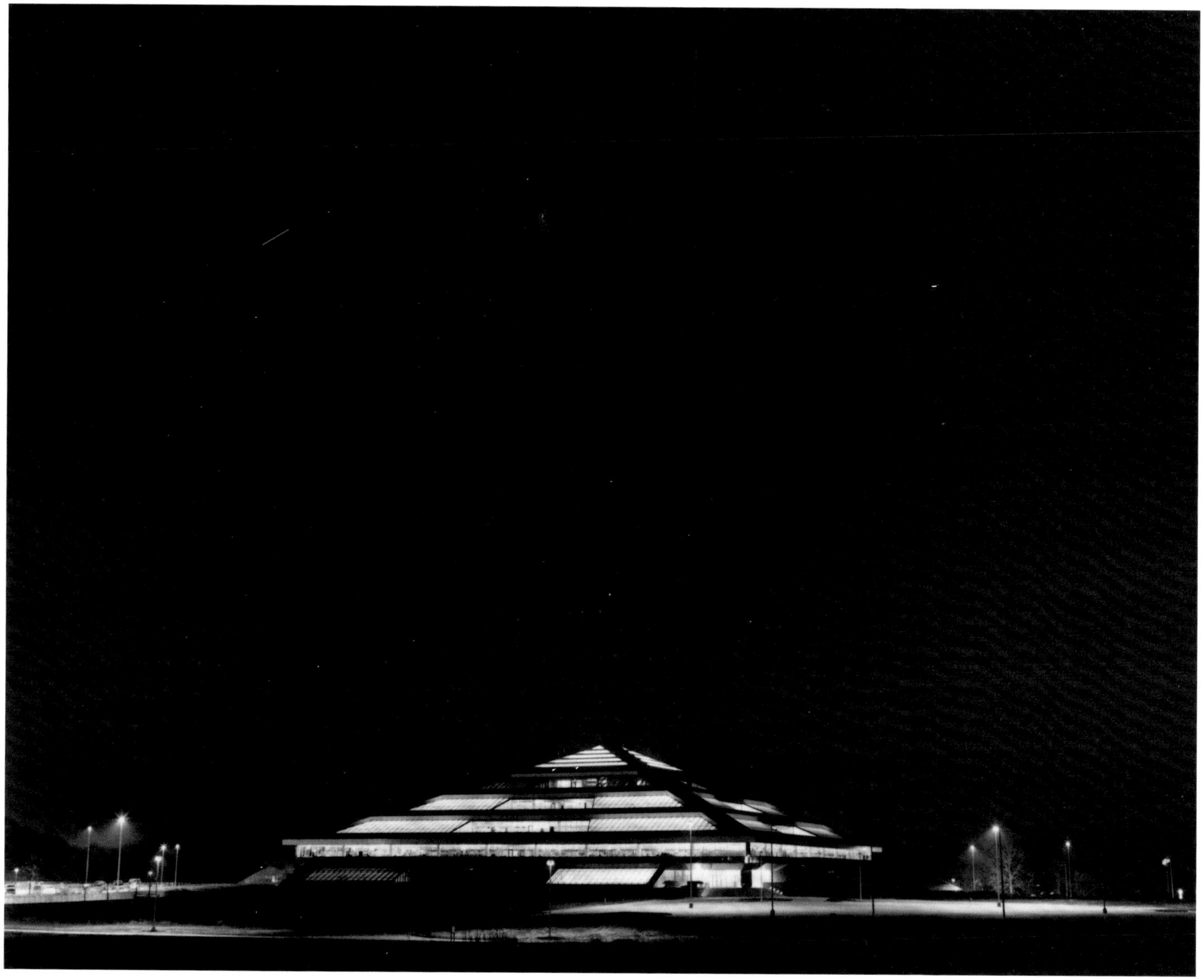

plate twenty-three   Plaza Towers, 2000

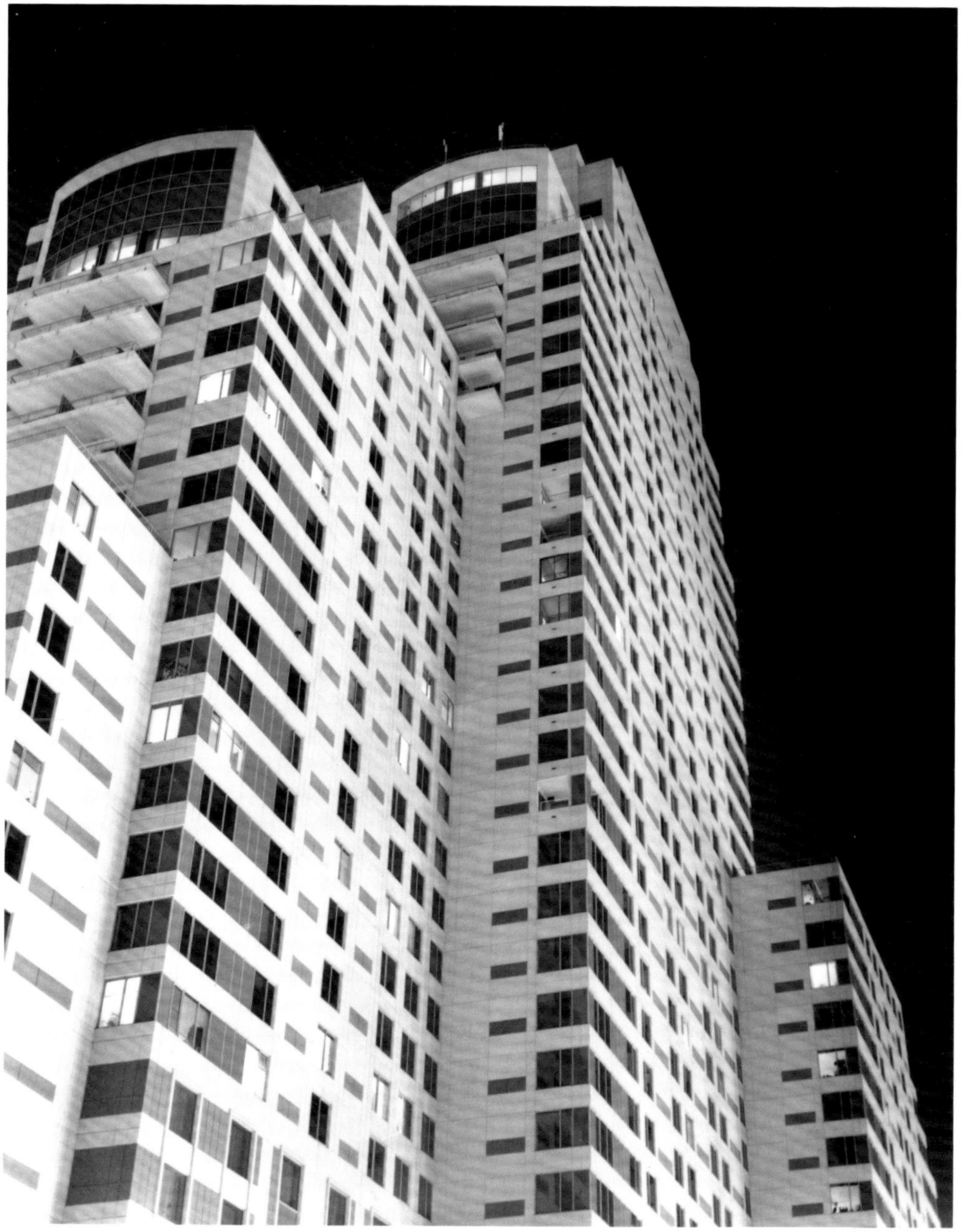

plate twenty-four   Moonlit Path - Frederik Meijer Gardens, 2000

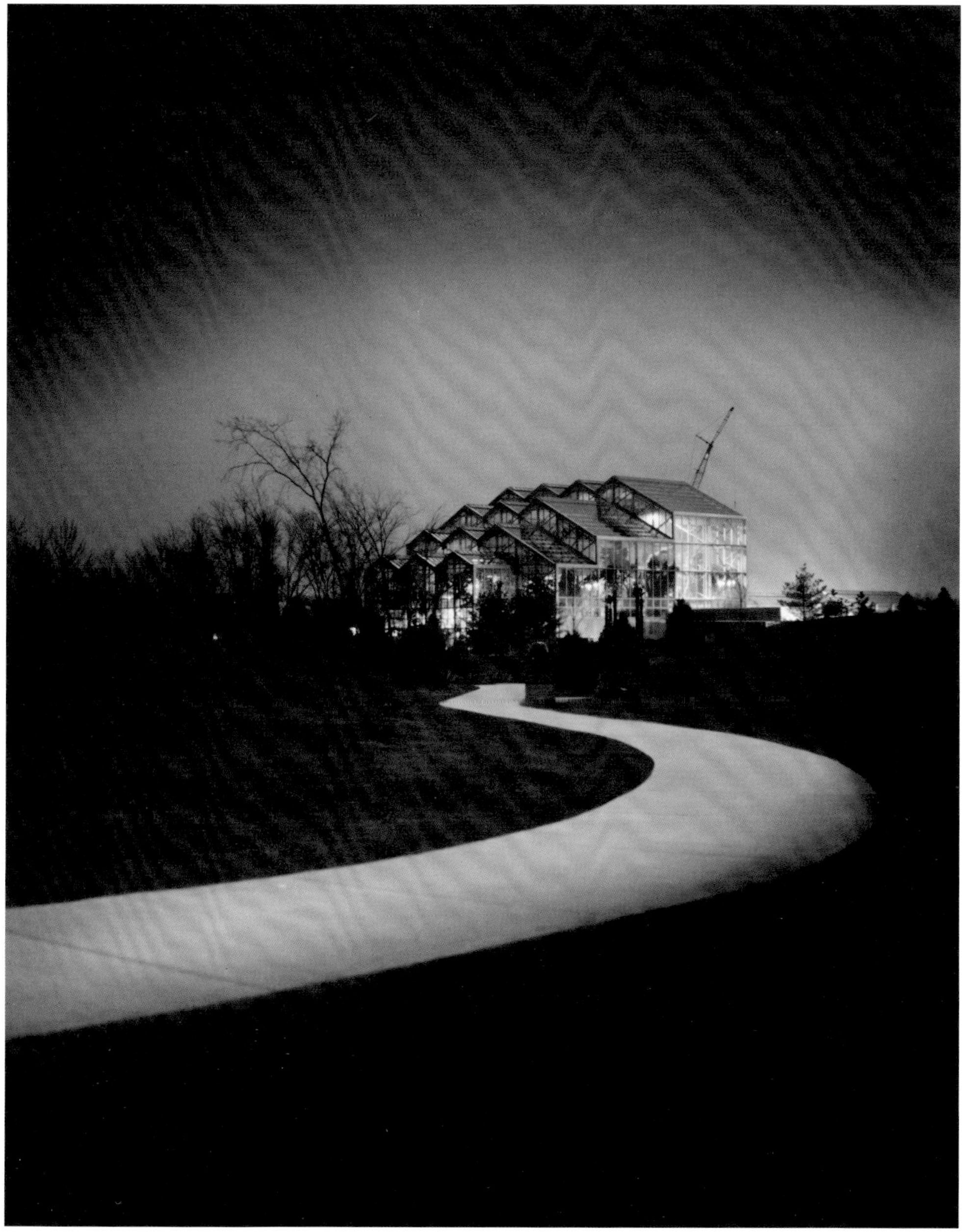

plate twenty-five   Moonlit Horse - Frederik Meijer Gardens, 2000

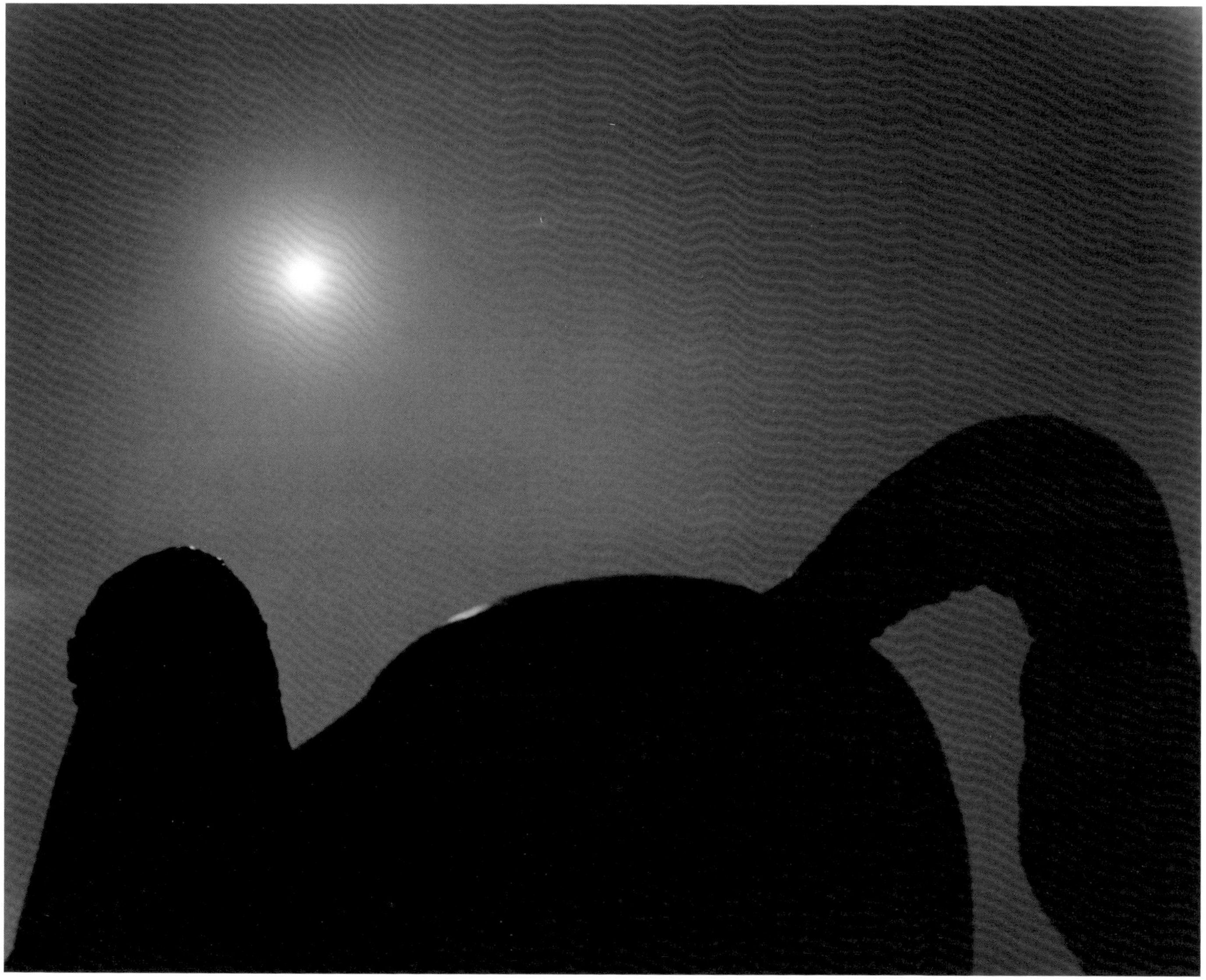

plate twenty-six   Two Trees, Horse's Tail - Frederik Meijer Gardens, 2000

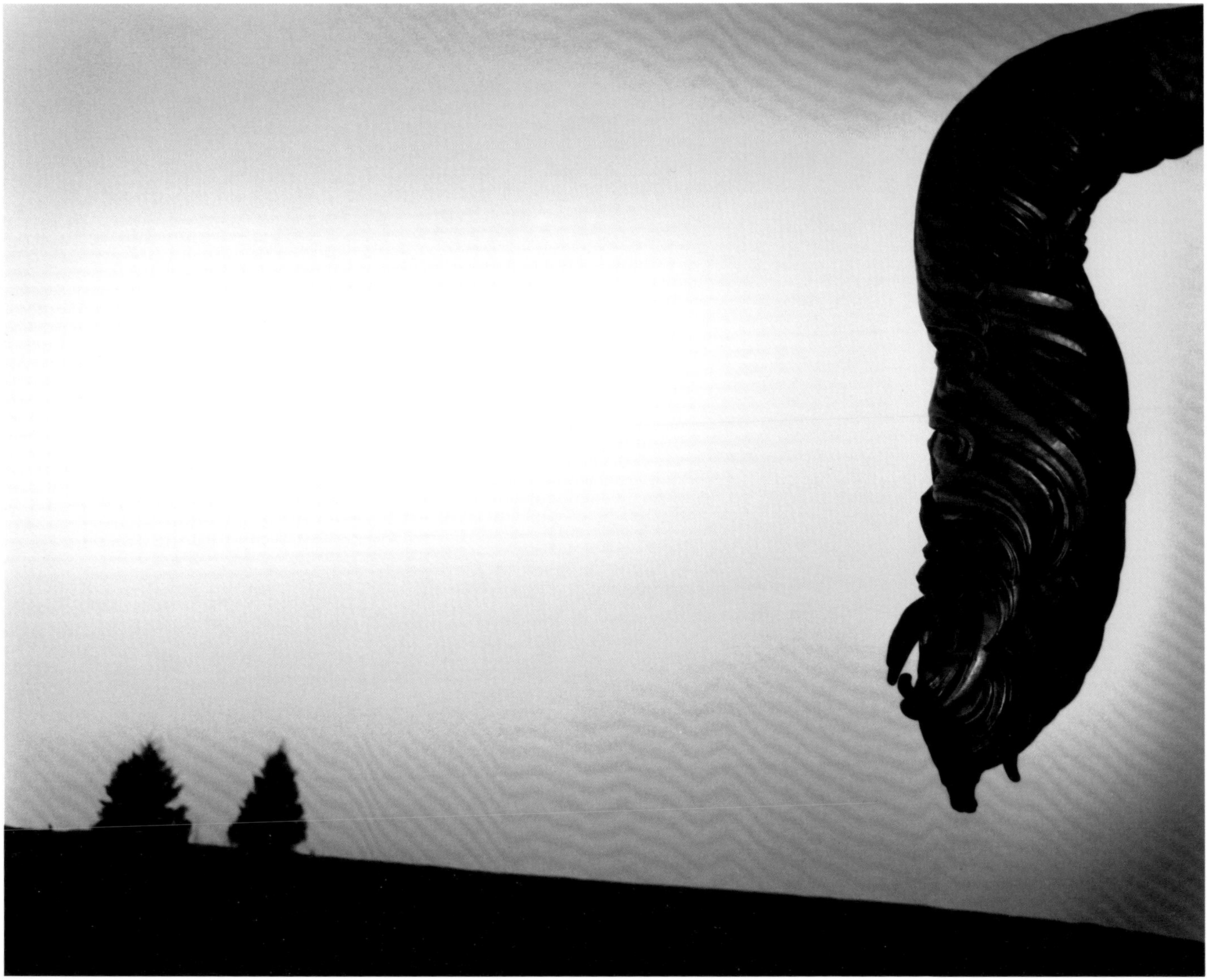

plate twenty-seven    Night Gargoyle - Opus 1894, 2000

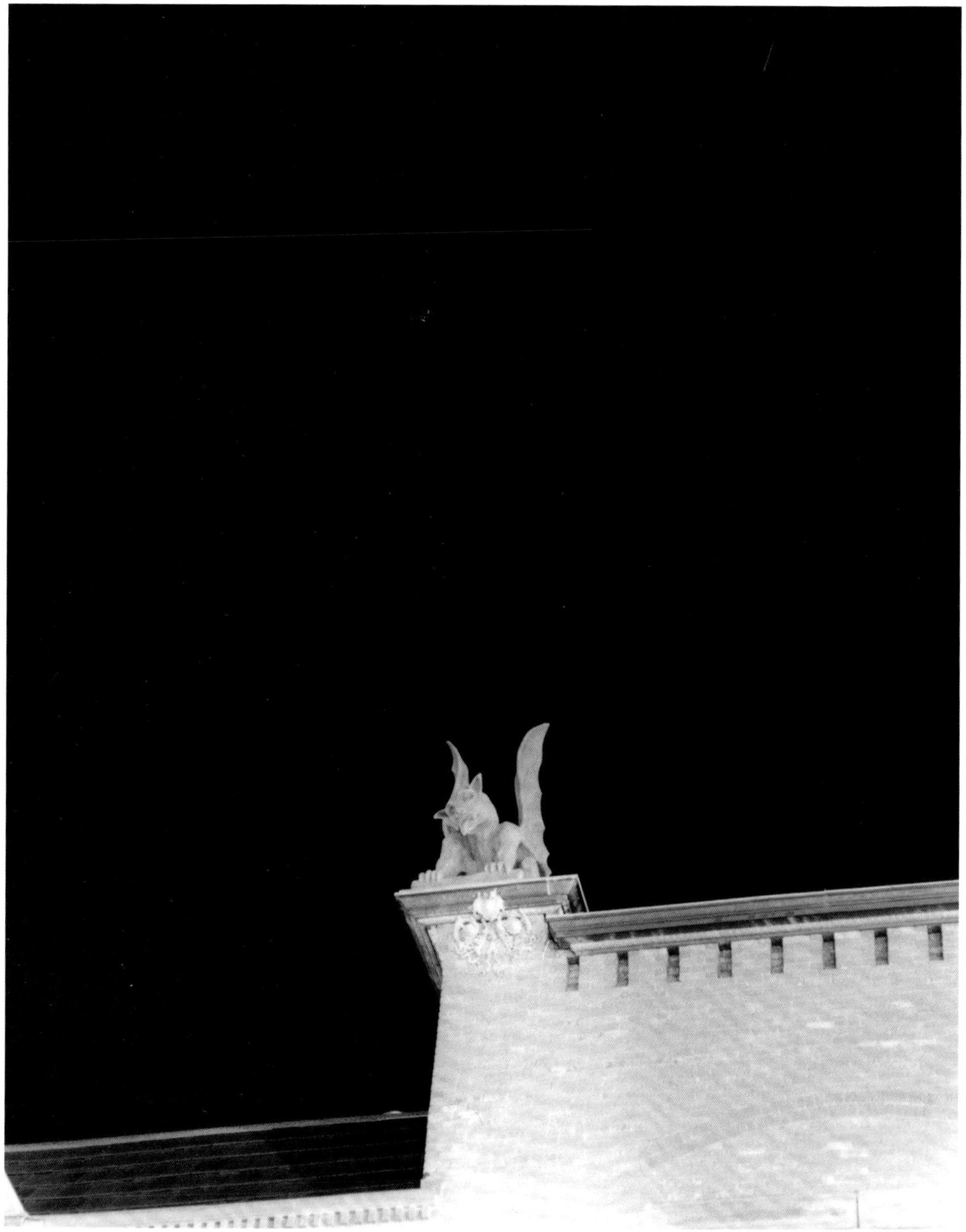

plate twenty-eight   Guardian Angel - Marywood, 2000

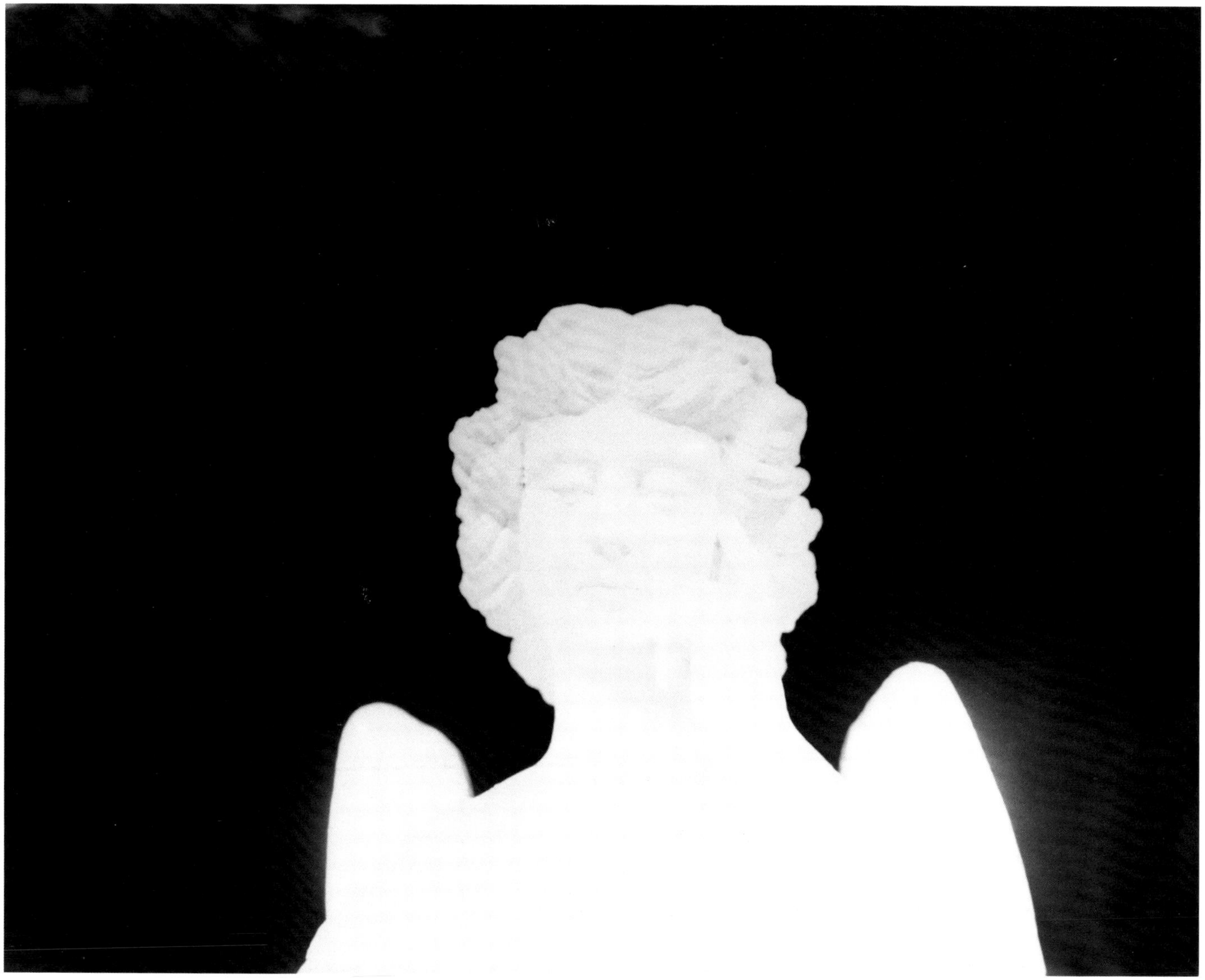

# Amplified Plate List

1. River Arches (1998) - Gillett Bridge spans the Grand River from the Gerald R. Ford Museum to the Welsh Auditorium and Amway Grand Plaza Hotel.

2. River Abstract (1998) - Photographed in front of the Gerald R. Ford Museum, a long exposure of the passing waters of the Grand River creates interesting forms.

3. Fish Ladder, Sixth Street Bridge (1996) - The foreground in this image looks much different during the day when fisherman crowd onto the rocks.

4. South View One (1996) - Since exhibiting this photograph in college photography class, it has become a widely known work by the photographer.

5. Lamp Post - Van Andel Public Museum (1998)

6. Calder Abstract (2000) - This huge steel sculpture, called *La Grande Vitesse*, was created by noted sculpture artist Alexander Calder.

7. Glowing Pillars - Bridgewater Place (2000) - This is the only office building on the west side of the Grand River containing high-rise Class A office space.

8. Steam Cloud, Star Trails - Bridgewater Place (2000)

9. Crescent Moon and Van Andel Arena (1996)

10. Van Andel Arena - Aerial (1998) - Photographed from the top of the Plaza Towers Building.

11. Van Andel Public Museum - Aerial (1998) - Photographed from the top of the Plaza Towers Building, this building contains the Grand Rapids Public Museum.

12. Under Pearl Street Bridge and Van Andel Museum (2000)

13. Six Trees - Van Andel Institute (2000) - Looming behind the trees in Crescent Park is the Van Andel Institute, a new cancer research facility spearheaded by the Van Andel family's philanthropic efforts.

14. Nine Flags - Amway World Headquarters (2000) - These flags stand in front of Amway World Headquarters in Ada.

15. Lamp Post, Covered Bridge - Ada (2000) - This historic covered bridge is located in the village of Ada.

16. Tree and Blue Bridge (2000) - The Blue Bridge is a pedestrian bridge that spans the river connecting Grand Valley State University's Downtown campus and Plaza Towers.

17. Illuminated Trees - Collins Park, EGR (2000) - These trees stand in Collins Park on the shore of Reeds Lake in East Grand Rapids. A passing plane can be seen on the left side of the image.

18. Wet Sidewalk - Gerald R. Ford Museum (1998)

19. Five Arches (1999) - Gillett Bridge connects the Welsh Auditorium and the Gerald R. Ford Museum.

20. Passing Bike and Monroe Café (2000) - A cyclist passes through this long exposure, leaving a trail of blinking lights from the bike's taillight. Streaks of light left by passing cars fill the right side of the image.

21. Moon and Amway Grand Plaza Hotel (2000) - This hotel may be the most identifiable building in the City's growing skyline.

22. Star Trails and Steelcase Pyramid (2000) - Located near the airport, this building is unmistakable and a wonderful piece of architecture.

23. Plaza Towers (2000) - The tallest building in Grand Rapids at thirty-four floors, it contains a hotel, retail shops (including the photographer's gallery), apartments and luxury condominiums.

24. Moonlit Path - Frederik Meijer Gardens (2000) - This sculpture and garden park is the result of the philanthropic efforts of local businessman Frederik Meijer and many community volunteers.

25. Moonlit Horse - Frederik Meijer Gardens (2000) - Silhouetted against a full moon, this massive bronze horse is one of only two in the world created by noted sculptor Nina Akamu.

26. Two Trees, Horse's Tail - Frederik Meijer Gardens (2000)

27. Night Gargoyle - Opus 1894 (2000) - This gargoyle stands guard on top of Opus 1894, a nightclub and restaurant in the resurgent "Old Town" district of downtown Grand Rapids.

28. Guardian Angel - Marywood (2000) - Dominican Center at Marywood.

# Biography

Born in 1968, Brian Kelly is a lifelong resident of Grand Rapids, Michigan. His professional career began at the age of twenty-seven, after two years of study in a concentrated photography program in Grand Rapids. In a relatively short period of time, Kelly has established himself as an accomplished artist working in the medium of photography. His fine art photography is found in many important collections, both public and private.

Kelly's work is not easily categorized. It is rooted in the abstract and his unique compositions create interesting juxtapositions. Kelly's images reflect his passion for architecture and love of the nocturnal photograph. Kelly is fascinated by the interaction of the night and long exposures; believing that light accumulating on film over time can express qualities impossible to see with the naked eye. His singular style has garnered praise and acceptance in the artistic community, his work most recently having been accepted into the Grand Rapids Art Museum.

In 1998, responding to the demand for his fine art black and white work, Brian, and his wife Kathleen, opened a gallery in the heart of downtown Grand Rapids called bkGallery. Located in the Plaza Towers Building, this art gallery is the first in the area to show exclusively black and white photography. The gallery focuses on sales to individual collectors and corporations, always attempting to educate and cultivate enthusiasm for collecting photographic prints.

Kelly's award-winning commercial work is architecturally and advertising based, most recently winning a prestigious Addy Award. His specialty is photographing interiors and exteriors of buildings for a variety of clients, including architects, interior designers, construction firms and several magazines. His world travels are chronicled in a travel column he writes for each issue of *Grand Rapids Cosmopolitan Home Magazine*.

Contact Information
bkGallery and Brian Kelly Photography
29 Monroe Ave.
Grand Rapids, MI 49503
phone: 616.224.2700
fax: 616.224.2701
web site: www.briankellyphoto.com
e-mail: gallery@briankellyphoto.com

To order books or inquire about fine art photography publishing projects, please contact:
Glass Eye
P.O. Box 1811
Grand Rapids, MI 49501-1811
616.246.5163

Brian Kelly's photographs may also be purchased at:
The Grand Rapids Art Museum
Sales and Rental Gallery
155 N. Division
Grand Rapids, MI 49503
616.831.2922

## Collecting Information

All images presented on these pages are available for purchase. Each photograph is printed in a limited edition of thirty (with the exception of Plate Four in this book which has an edition of forty-five). Standard print size is 11" x 14". All prints are personally printed by Brian Kelly on fiber base paper and processed to strict archival standards. The print is then archivally mounted and overmatted with acid-free board to an overall dimension of 20" x 22". Larger print sizes are available by special request and priced accordingly. All prints are signed and titled by the artist on the overmatte. An additional signature and individual print information is recorded on the photographer's stamp on the verso of the mount. The availability and price of a specific image is subject to prior sales of that image. Contact the gallery for the current price of each image you are interested in purchasing.

A special collector's edition, consisting of a complete set of the photographs in this book and presented in a special collector's case, is also available. Please contact the gallery for pricing and more specific information.